MW01119697

GOBOS FOR IMAGE PROJECTION

Michael Hall
Julie Harper

ENTERTAINMENT TECHNOLOGY PRESS

Reference Series

Front cover image – Cyrano de Bergerac 1994.
Lighting design: David Hersey, Photo: Wyatt Enever

GOBOS FOR IMAGE PROJECTION

Michael Hall and Julie Harper

Entertainment Technology Press

Gobos for Image Projection

© Michael Hall and Julie Harper

First edition published September 2010
by Entertainment Technology Press Ltd
The Studio, High Green, Great Shelford, Cambridge CB22 5EG
Internet: www.etnow.com

ISBN 978 1 904031 62 8

A title within the
Entertainment Technology Press Reference Series
Series editor: John Offord

CODE / GIP01-09/10

PREFACE

This is essentially a reference book outlining the history, technical developments and uses of gobos. It is not our intention to try and teach how to use gobos creatively.

For this we had a better idea: we would leave this to the professionals and invite lighting designers from around the world to contribute a few words on how and why they use gobos in their chosen field.

Initially we asked for a small 100 word contribution from each, which explains some of the concise and disciplined replies. But as the idea developed our contributors' offerings expanded similarly! We delighted in the variety of replies and felt all had valuable thoughts to share. We now share them with you in full, interspersed through the chapters of this book.

So, we would like to extend our thanks to the many designers from Japan, Hong Kong, Australia, Europe and the USA for their ready help who, we feel, have added more colour and depth to a book we hope you will also find interesting and instructional.

Michael Hall and Julie Harper

6 Gobos for Image Projection

FOREWORD

Today we light our stages with multiple cones of often-coloured light, which converge to surround the actor with illumination that hopefully reveals, creates atmosphere, and helps tell the story.

It wasn't always like that. For centuries, candlelight, oil, and gas provided only soft general illumination.

Between the two World Wars, the great English director, Basil Dean, after a lifetime supporting technical innovation, including importing the first baby spotlight into England, became convinced by the potential in truly soft light ... reflected light. I've tried to follow his intent, but always hated the result. Reflected soft-light goes everywhere ... I have always wanted to direct the audience's attention to the performer.

But cones? Cones seem boring.

And thus to me, the gobo becomes one of the really useful tools in the lighting designer's palette. The ability to texture light, to make it playful, unexpected, mottled ... alive – now that is fun!

I think I began with multiple colours in a single frame to provide texture. Offsetting the reflector in a plano-convex spotlight could be exciting too. In England, when the Patt. 23 at last emerged, to emulate the American ellipsoidal, the way opened up for gobos.

Of course, gobos do all the obviously literal stuff: light through windows, New York fire escapes, moon and clouds, water ripple, these can all support location, place-finding. But it is the texture of light that has always interested me. And this is the gobo's strength.

Light in nature shifts about a lot. This week on a sunlit day in the Connecticut woods, I watch sunlight through trees. The patterns wondrously change shape, rolling from soft to hard focus, with myriad beams dancing and twirling through the dusty air. Magic!

We are after magic on our stages ... magic light to surround living actors. Gobos are a valuable step forward. Pattern projection by video is the start of a more lively capability for textured light. The future holds much promise.

Michael Hall and Julie Harper have written the definitive book on all you want to know about the gobo. I'm happy to have played a small role in the story; happy that I encouraged Stan Miller to bring Rosco to the UK; happy too, to have chained a youthful David Hersey to the bench at Theatre Projects, hand-cutting gobos. His, and others' suffering has helped change our world of stage lighting.

Richard Pilbrow

CONTENTS

ACKNOWLEDGEMENTS

We would like to thank the contributors who shared their knowledge, memories and expertise with us in the writing of this book. Notably, and in no particular order, David Hersey, Wyatt Enever, Vicky Fairall, Joel Nichols, Jim Bornhorst, Claus Hansen, Simon Allan, Francis Reid, Jules Fisher, Stan Miller, David Robertson, Ben M Rogers, Joe Tawil, Mike Wood and, of course, Richard Pilbrow who has written the Foreword.

A special thanks goes to Julie Cheung, our graphic designer who kept her head while we were losing ours!

A special thanks also to Jackie Staines who produced this book from our manuscript and images in phenomenal time.

INTRODUCTION

Gobos, or images for projection, exist today in a wide range of physical sizes, on a variety of substrates with ever increasing diversity of image designs.

The number of projectors for gobos continues to increase and diversify from a small LED sourced projector, to the high wattage of tungsten halogen and discharge lamps.

The quality of projection optics continues to improve, which demands higher resolution quality of gobos – and, in turn, spurs manufacturers to better universal projector quality.

The designer and audience reap the benefit of this continuous change.

This book tracks the early provenance of our technology from early Magic Lantern design roots, through the concentrated period of development during the 1960s, to the state of the art gobos that we use today in 2010.

It also gives a fundamental guide to gobo types, usage and some of the accessories available to the designer.

It is clear that updated editions will be needed, from this snapshot of today.

The Provenance of the word 'Gobo'

What is a 'gobo' and where did the name derive?

This account is drawn from many correspondents.

Francis Reid suggests: "A template placed in a spotlight to texture the light or to project a silhouette outline" and thinks the word 'gobo' must have been in use in the early '60s. In 1963 the plans for Martin Walser's *The Rabbit Race* showed 'G' for Strand Pattern 53s and 23s, along with Cinemoid 38 and 50, to 'dapple' a set with a big tree centre piece.

In the USA, Stanley McCandless and Eldon Elder both used the word 'gobo' in 1962. Others describe 'Leko patterns', or 'Leko template projections'. Jules Fisher describes 'patterns with ellipsoidal' and another 'template with 1000W 8" Leko'.

The word was, and is, also used in the film industry, with evidence as far back as 1934 when it was described in terms of a framing shutter ellipsoidal fixture eliminating the need for 'gobo-lights shields'.

There are also arguments for its naming being derived from the large cut-outs used in film where the DP might say: "This 'goes between' the 2kw Fresnel and the actor," which was then shortened to 'gobo'.

Still more suggestions might be:

Goes Before Optics – which perhaps, literally, should be 'goes in optics' – as opposed to a 'cookie' which goes after optics.

Or short for 'Go Between'.

One thing is for certain, there seems to be no definitive explanation for the term 'gobo', but their popularity as an indispensible tool for lighting designers is undeniable.

On one show, lit by Francis Reid, gobos were so prevalent that the show became known by the stage crew as *Anne of Green Gobos*!

HISTORY

Durham Marenghi
Lighting Designer, UK: Theatre,
Opera, Dance, Trade, Heritage,
Concert, Television.

I use gobos in five distinct ways:
as a way to break up stage
lighting into dappled or geometric
patterns, as a connection
between the light source or
lighting rig architecture to
splinter the beams and create a
contrasting physical effect visible
in haze, to transform scenic or
architectural surfaces into something unnatural, to create ripples of
light as fixtures move across our audiences and to create beams in
the air around and about an audience to draw them into our world.

1 A BRIEF HISTORY OF 250 YEARS OF PROJECTION 1646-1910

There are two special eras of intense development activity for projection: here we review a brief history of the first era, ending just 100 years ago, at 1910, before dealing with the later era in Chapter 2 which starts in 1960 with what we now call 'gobos'.

In our research we find that many technical innovations of the last 50 years were anticipated and achieved by inventive engineers and showmen in the late nineteenth century.

The latter part of this period saw a world-wide explosion of ingenious development and marketing of a mass entertainment – we'll call it the Magic Lantern time – which flourished until the development of cinematography caused its decline.

The monk Athanasius Kircher is generally regarded as the father of Magic Lantern technology. He wrote in 1646 about his projection work using rectangular slides and a simple convex-lensed projector, with sunlight or candlelight as the light source, to project simple images, including a clock and a hand.

We can condense our summary to some separate elements:

> **Light Sources**
> **Slides**
> **Lanterns**
> **Photography & Cinematography**
> **State of the Business**

Light Sources
The introduction of electricity and the tungsten filament lamp revolutionised projection, but there was a progression of other sources before this.

Candles
Candles were little used in projection, as they were of low intrinsic brightness, tended to flicker and smoke, and the actual flame lowered in

burning, although springs were devised to keep the flame in a constant position.

Oil

Although oil lamps were used from early times, there were many disadvantages.

Initially whale oil was used, and then fish oil, which was refined principally from the livers of cod, herring and hake, but it gave an offensive smell when burned and produced little light.

Roman period oil lamps.

Vegetable oil was preferred, and by the 1870s paraffin (called kerosene in the US) had largely replaced the traditional oils.

To overcome the low light levels, three or four woven wick burners were used.

In the late eighteenth century, François-Pierre-Ami Argand developed a circular wick mounted between two concentric glass cylinders. The resulting flame was whiter and bright and, being draught-free, was a steady source.

Camphor could be added to the oil to increase the flame brightness.

Acetylene

The great English chemist, Sir Humphrey Davy, discovered acetylene.

This is a gas that is generated from a block of calcium carbide when heated. Acetylene gas burned with a bright, steady and smokeless flame. It was a stable process and was used for small portable projectors and for the lamps of 'horseless carriages'.

Limelight

A word happily still with us colloquially, limelight produces an intense white light when a block of lime is heated by flame from a mixture of oxygen and hydrogen gas. This high brightness light source gave new impetus to the Magic Lantern, especially larger lanterns with a long throw projecting large images in theatres or buildings with large audiences.

This was demonstrated first in 1825 and its effective useful life as a popular light source stretched from 1838 for Magic Lanterns, through the turn of the century into the early years of film.

An industry sprang up, offering supplies of lime blocks, or lime cartridges. The gas mixture was contained in bags, (which were liable to be punctured by mischievous boys) and later in separate iron cylinders, which were colour coded for easy identification. Unfortunately the standard colours were different in the US and England!

The introduction of coal gas permitted piped coal gas to replace hydrogen.

Coal Gas

Coal gas was demonstrated in the London Lyceum theatre in 1789, and by 1817 was in wide use for theatre lighting, but because of its low brightness, was not widely used for Magic Lanterns, except for domestic use where a small image size was acceptable.

Carbon Arc

Greater light output was achieved with the development of the carbon arc. A small separation between two carbon rods, with a DC electric current applied, gives a high density arc.

This was used as a source for big lanterns, with DC power provided by bulky batteries and, in 1844, used in Paris for a projecting microscope. Because of its high intensity and compact nature, carbon arcs were used extensively in film projection and searchlights.

Electricity

In 1879, Edison in the US and Joseph Swan in England both made an electrically powered filament lamp and by 1890 most major theatres were lit by electricity, usually with each theatre having its own generating plant in the basement.

Initially the big loop filament of the lamps were not useful for the Magic Lantern, but the Edison Swann Company soon brought out a flat plane square grid of filament, about ½" square.

Early filament lamp – note big filament, not compact.

By 1911 tungsten was used as the filament, and an efficiency of 9 lumens/Watt achieved.

So in 1910 when the London Palladium was opened, it was lit by electricity, powering battens with three colour circuits and 18 carbon arc 'searchlights'. Modernity had arrived!

Slides

Many aspects in the development of projection slides are echoed in the later development of gobos. For the earliest projectors, glass was an ideal stable carrier for an image.

A standard size of 3¼" (8.25 cm) square was adopted in the 19th Century – although there were variants.

In the early days, the image was hand painted. By 1830, transfer printing was adapted from ceramic printing and multiple production became easy.

Mid 19ᵗʰ century 3¼" glass slide.

In 1839 Fox Talbot made advances in the photographic process and by 1847 photographs could be printed on glass.

The monotone images could be hand tinted and an industry sprang up, centred in Covent Garden in central London. Initially there was no good transparent red dye. With almost mass production of slides, sets of slides

A religious slide.

Image of Crystal Palace.

were produced – still very collectable today – on a range of subjects, and sheets of notes issued. Many of these were educational and worthy.

The great American showman, Robertson, developed 'phantasmagoria' (literally meaning 'ghostly apparitions'). He pioneered the technique of making an opaque black surround to his slides, instead of the usual clear edge surround, so that when his images were projected on a screen or on to smoke, the image seemed to float.

Some slides were circular, and mounted in hardwood frames, with wooden tracks to enable easy slide change and good registration to hold focus.

19ᵗʰ century multiple image slide and panoramic image. 3¼" glass slide.

The illustrations of Kircher's 1646 Treatise on Projection show rectangular glass with several circular images and this practice became very popular in the mid 1800s, both with separate images and a continuous landscape which could be slid through the gate.

Dissolving Views

Using two lanterns side-by-side, or one mounted directly over another, it was possible to create dissolving views.

This could be done by projecting similar images, but with key differences, carefully lined up to be in perfect registration.

The cross-fade change was achieved in one of several ways: an early method was to manually raise or lower the wick in the oil burner, but more commonly a serrated 'flag' or a rotating wheel was used.

To help make smooth changes a third projector was often mounted forming a triple unit, known then as a triunial.

Two lanterns with crossfade semaphore arm.

Dissolve for seamless change from night to day.

Motion Effects

In the last 50 years of the nineteenth century, there was a flood of inventions for slides to simulate movement or dynamic effects. There are more than 20 classifications of types – too many to review in detail – but it is clear that much of today's advanced technology for moving lights was anticipated nearly one hundred years ago.

One of the movement techniques was to mount two slides in one wooden frame, one fixed and one moveable – a subject set on the fixed glass and the 'slipping glass' depicting say an arm, produces the apparent movement. Both glasses could slide giving more complex motion. Nearly all of these techniques rely on persistence of vision.

As projection quality improved, there was a demand for higher quality slides and the improved detailing of transfer printing and photographic quality images demanded better projection technology – a similar position today.

The first moving light animation – dancing skeletons.

Lanterns

A lantern is a device to house the light source and optimise the light output through a series of reflector and lenses to ultimately project an image.

By the nineteenth century lantern design became a serious business.

For the simplest forms, the body was fabricated from tin, usually painted black or decorated artistically.

Larger bodies were constructed from sheet iron with Russian sheet iron most commonly used. The ore was mined in the Urals and the sheets were smooth and polished.

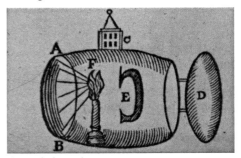

An early basic lantern.

Then there was a fashion for elegant wood, usually a stained mahogany, with a tin lining inside and an all brass front. The front carried runners for good slide registration.

The early lenses were a single biconverse lens which gave poor focus across the whole plane (spherical aberration). This was solved before 1800 by the use of a double condenser lens, giving a clearer and sharper picture. Colour fringing (chromatic aberration) was resolved in 1840 by the development of achromatic lenses, a mixture of crown and flint glass.

To reduce heat, an early 'heatshield' was used either to protect the lenses, or the slides: a glass trough was interposed containing alum solution, which absorbed some infrared energy, while still passing light.

Another pleasing invention was a device to ensure the screen was never blank (shame about the Kodak Carousel). This was made possible by sliding the incoming slide to the projecting position as the previous one falls back out of focus and then out of the light path.

Many variants of the basic lantern were developed, from the projecting microscope of great size and weight, down to small portable toys.

Photography and Cinematography

Early work on the photographic image started in 1822, and by 1840, Fox Talbot had developed it into an art form.

A toy lantern and oil sourced projector.

By 1860 a camera was developed with four lenses, each filtered and recorded. A four-lens projector was used with corresponding filters, but it was cumbersome and fell into disuse.

Maxwell demonstrated that the colours red, green and blue light could be synthesised and images coincided to create an almost realistic image.

Curiously, 100 years later the experiment was repeated at Eastman Kodak, and it was found that the plates that Maxwell used were in fact insensitive to red light. Luckily the red fabrics used reflected ultraviolet radiation, which the red plate was sensitive to, so it did, by chance, work.

Motion pictures had their origins in the late 1870s. In 1877 24 still photographs were taken of a galloping horse with the horse tripping threads that activated a battery of cameras.

By the early 1890s a system arrived, developed by Edison, where a continuous 35 mm film, perforated on the two edges, moved to show 46 frames per second behind a viewing aperture. This achieved popularity as a penny in the slot machine and is the undisputed original of the standard width of film and perforation detail.

In 1895, in Paris, the Lumiere brothers demonstrated their 'Cinematographie' apparatus, which could take and project moving pictures.

Early film in theatre.

By 1910 Léon Gaumont had mastered the technique of recording sound and images simultaneously and demonstrated to the Academy of Sciences in Paris.

So it was from this point that the popularity of the Magic Lantern, and all its intricate mechanisms for dissolves and movement, began to wane – but not to disappear – coexisting alongside film for at least two decades.

Combination shows of moving pictures and Magic Lanterns were common, slides were used for advertising, and as interludes to let the operator change reels.

State of the Business

There were many enthusiastic users, showmen and businesses in the latter years of the nineteenth century, and in 1890 the Lantern Society was formed in London under the chairmanship of The Hon. Slingsby Bethell, CB.

Some of its aims were to promote exhibitions of 'general scientific interest' to encourage members to make loans of their collections to others.

The first exhibition was to show 150 lantern slides, about art, science and recreation, using a lantern converted to use 'electric light' as the illuminant.

John Barnes has researched a list of Magic Lantern manufacturers in this period, and there are over 100 entries.

Nearly all of the lantern manufacturers showed twin or triple lanterns for dissolving views.

The slide sets publicised included narrative stories with much of the production including poems, ballads and popular songs.

The Magic Lantern was the television of the day. There were variants, such as the Panorama – a 360° wall of a painting within a circular building, or rotunda – which became highly popular. The word 'panorama' sounds classical (it might have been good for IMAX), but was a word coined in 1791.

By 1900 there were 250 Panoramas in Europe alone. In Chicago the images could be projected from a central suspended position which carried an operator and eight lanterns mounted in a circle, sourced with carbon arcs.

Wyldes Great Globe – Leicester Square 1851.

Let us remind ourselves that all the technical ingenuity and strands of development leading to good quality projection, both static and with motion, depends on our ability to perceive colour, and our characteristic of persistence of vision, which enables us to see flicker free images when 24 frames per second are projected.

All of these techniques are important in the later development of gobos.

The Mysterious Image

The mysterious image: stare at the negative image for 20 seconds and then look at a blank wall surface, the positive after image will be seen.

Wendy Luedtke
Lighting Designer, USA: Theatre, Live Events, Architecture.

I use gobos to create illusion – shadows as if from objects that aren't really there – to transform location and time, to build depth and intrigue. I am fascinated with the ability to add an absence of light. I love finding just the right texture to shape both the light and the darkness. Jagged edges, feathery wisps, rigid angles, or organic curves – which one fits this world and supports the mood of this moment? As the shadows come to life, do I paint them with colour from other fixtures or let mystery saturate the void?

Paule Constable
Lighting Designer, UK: Theatre, Opera, Dance.

There can be nothing more beautiful than the light passing through the trees of a summer woodland, early in the morning when the dew is rising as mist and we see the extraordinary light carved out of the woody shade.

Recently I came across a charcoal burner working in a glade in one of our local woods; the smoke from his work was caught in the light and created an image so dramatic it made you want to weep.

The high windows in Grand Central station casting beams of light across the hurrying commuters.

All these scenes give real life a heightened quality; a theatricality we strive for. Our tool to recreate this in the theatre is the gobo. Gobos can be used to create images of equal grandeur and splendour as those I talk about BUT…too often they become a terrible theatrical shorthand. The light in a cobbled street is not cobbled – the surface the light hits is! What is interesting about the light coming from water is that it is reflected, soft, mottled. I don't negate the use of gobos in creating these effects – I just don't often find that they are really the answer!

In lighting what interests me is trying to push an idea to its purest form while still maintaining the performance. Try to take an idea back to its essential form. What happens if you actually bounce light off water? If the light passing through an object is beautiful then try to pass it through that object! Put a tree or a window on stage!

Obviously this isn't always possible. But gobos, while fantastic and a useful tool, can make us lazy in our ideas. Use them when they are the right thing to use, but always think about them, in fact any light in a show, with good rigorous thinking.

2 THE DEVELOPMENT HISTORY OF THE PRESENT DAY GOBO

The development of the concept of patterns or gobos and proliferation of designs is an interesting story, and involves many designers and lighting industry characters.

We've traced in Chapter 1 the ingenuity and diversity of effects created for the Magic Lantern, and inevitably there would be a crossover to theatre. In this chapter we will deal with how gobos came to be in the modern form we are more familiar with nowadays.

Development in Europe was obscure, but one story without conclusion is intriguing.

Richard Wagner controlled the technical detail of the design of his Festspielhaus in Bayreuth for his 13 operas: particularly guarding the acoustic resonance using bare boards without any sound damping carpet.

For *Parsifal*, premiered in July 1882, there was a call for an effect, referred to as 'Fleckenlicht'. Max Keller, who worked at Bayreuth in 1967, and tells us that the term is no longer in use, but did refer to gobos and projection, and that the word 'fleck' has multiple definitions – spots, fleck of paint, and dapples – but we don't know what Wagner's technicians created.

There's an intriguing gap in our knowledge about gobos in England before 1960.

We suspect that Joe Davis and Cyril Griffiths, both sadly passed away, and other ingenious people in the theatre probably were making gobos, by drilling and snipping metal, but we don't know.

We know that Arthur Miller's *Death of a Salesman* was premiered in New York in 1946, and in London in 1949 at the Phoenix Theatre, and that TABS published the lighting plans.

For the New York production Arthur Miller specified an effect projection for Spring and Autumn leaves. The lighting designer was Jo Mielziner. We suspect that this was achieved with patterns. The London production followed the lighting concepts of Jo Mielziner but was created by Joe Davis, who signed off the lighting plans as Joe Davis, Chief Engineer, H M Tennent Ltd.

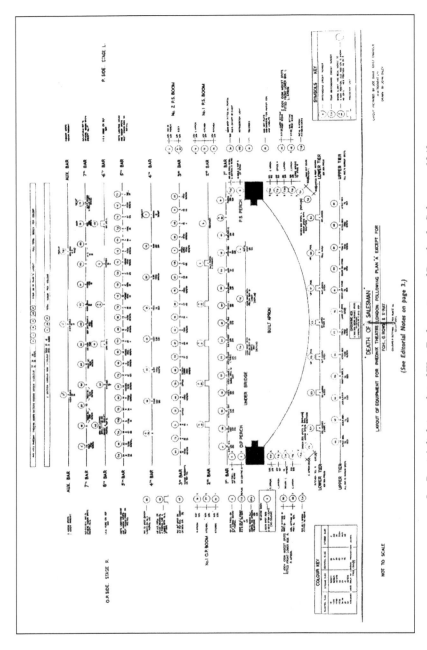

Joe Davis's lighting plot of West End premiere of Death of a Salesman - 1949

34 Gobos for Image Projection

(Perhaps it's a good moment to repeat Joe's immortal words, recalled by Michael Northen (at that period billed as 'Technical Adviser' for *The Prisoner* at The Globe Theatre) in his autobiography, at an early meeting of the newly formed ALD, (Association of Lighting Designers, early founders of which with Joe, were Michael Northen, Bill Bundy, Richard Pilbrow, Charlie Bristow and John Wyckham) when Joe reminded new members: "Don't you boys forget, it was Michael and me who started this lighting racket".)

Francis Reid's memories are sharp and we reproduce his response in full later, at the end of this chapter.

The main growth of gobo creation in England was around 1959/60. June Dandridge, the production manager at Glyndebourne, mentioned them to Francis Reid, whereupon Bill Bundy at Covent Garden explained that they were punching holes in metal plates which sat in spot profile gates to create a light 'dappling' effect.

Francis started to create them in the 1962 summer season at Glyndebourne. He used metal gobos or 'dapplers' in the gate of 1kW Strand Pattern 53s – four on each of the over-stage lighting bridges – for Debussy's opera *Pelleas et Melisande*.

Gobos then were usually formed from aluminium or pie dish aluminium – although zinc, copper and tin were sometimes used – since the aluminium could be cut with scissors and holes drilled easily.

Brian Legge reminds us that the lid of Benson and Hedges cigarette tins were useful too!

Richard Pilbrow thinks he first made break up gobos in a 1959 production of *The Darling Buds of May* at the Saville Theatre, London and also for a very short production at the Lyric Hammersmith, in 1960, of *Wreath for Udomo* where he created lots of jungle. This had rear projection too but closed mid-way through opening night on account of the leading man reputedly being under the influence of something!

Gobo use continued to grow with Richard Pilbrow using them again for *As You Like It* at the Royal Shakespeare Theatre and later at the Aldwych starring Vanessa Redgrave in June '61 while Jo Aveline remarks on the prolific use of dappled light gobos for the *Royal Hunt of the Sun* at Chichester in 1964.

Robert Bryan adds a human touch to these designer aspirations and achievements: in the early days he remembers Pilbrow calling for two kinds of gobos for the production of *Peer Gynt* at the Old Vic – ordinary break ups ('roundish') and a 'Pine Tree' style. This was an absolute nightmare on the fingers and hands requiring much fine treatment involving drills and needle files and he "still has the scars from cutting and filing gobos". But apparently it worked well and several pints of ale followed to soften the hard work.

Pilbrow gathered a collection of lighting designers at Theatre Projects, including Robert Ornbo, Charlie Bristow and in 1967, David Hersey. David would hand cut gobos in the Neals Yard store, and maybe the labour intensive nature of that was an early inspiration for him to find a way to make gobos in a more efficient way, which of course he was later to do.

In mainland Europe there seems to be less information of the early days. German designer and directors' preference seems to have been for sharply defined beams and little use of break-ups, but the Dutch theatre had closer links with English design culture and Henk Van der Geest, who worked for Netherlands Opera, remembers Charlie Bristow specifying break up gobos in the seventies. Some of these were made by Henk using 1mm thick aluminium whilst others, such as sharp break ups, were jigsawed and lasted well.

Gobo Projectors

The Strand Pattern 23 Spotlight was developed in 1951, with shutter facility for cinema use, especially to frame the ice cream girl. It was developed further in 1953 for lighting the organ pipes in the Festival Hall. This ability to frame and focus was to prove the ideal starting point for gobo projection.

From the Strand stable (later Rank Strand) came the Patts 263 and 264.

CCT added impetus to gobo use in the late sixties with the launch of their Silhouette range. These gave a good flat field in projection and helped advance the use of gobos in television.

The Early Patt 23 500w 1952

ATV Studio 5 Wembley panoramic gobo effects by cut-outs – Bill Lee

The image above shows an ATV Studio 5 production at Wembley, by lighting designer Bill Lee, who arranged an effective panorama of cut-out images using Strand Patts 93s.

In the USA, there seems to be a greater knowledge of the early years. Much of what we learned was anecdotal, from the people who played a part in this technology, and it involves developments in tungsten lamps, reflector and lens technology

In 1932, Herbert Kleigl of Kleigl Brothers was experimenting with different reflector contours, for units to light the Radio City Theatres in New York. In 1934 Kleigl introduced an ellipsoidal spotlight, which included iris shutters and vertical and horizontal framing shutters, the basic principles of which came from a down light fixture developed by GE for the Radio City Music Hall.

Tungsten lamps, which by this time were becoming the preferred light source for filmmaking with sound, rather than noisy arc lamps, presented a problem because of their large filaments. Westinghouse then introduced a biplanar filament lamp, which was used with the filament plane sideways. GE produced a range of lamps up to 2kW, base up.

We quote Bill Klages' recollection: "The biggest problem was the availability of instruments that had good enough performance to work for television. All ellipsoidals available at that time for use in theatre had very poor performance for image projection, particularly in the larger studios.

"In black and white days, the best we had was an ellipsoidal 2kW fixture made by Kliegl. It came in two spreads, 1:2 and 1:3, or approximately 30 and 20 degrees. In colour we used a monstrous instrument by the same manufacturer, but with a 3kW lamp and a fan that had a tendency to emit loud screeching noises at inappropriate times. It

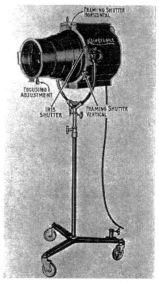

First potential gobo projector – Kleiglight 1934.

also had a most disappointing and very erratic performance as well.

"Things became better with the introduction of the 2kW Molelipso by Mole-Richardson, a well designed substitute based upon the Kleigl 2kW that made projections work in the larger venue applications. The unit made its introduction late 1970s. It was made at the request of Leard Davis who was a very fine lighting director who worked at CBS-Hollywood."

Then Bill Klages recalls: "All of the musical shows at the time were basically cyclorama based and the studios that I worked in were both high, 30-40 feet, and wide, about 80 feet.

"Like all working LDs, I had my supply of blanks of industrial grade of thick aluminium foil, X-acto knives,

Kleiglight S1365 Iris shutter, potential gobo projector early forties.

The Perry Como show 1963 NBC in Black & White, but shot off the monitor – hand cut burst pattern from aluminium in a Kleigl 2kW 6" ellipsoidal – Bill Klages.

sharpened scribe and tiny scissors to create a gobo at a moment's notice. Very popular were the first clouds, the most successful of which were silk-screened half-tone on a heat resistant glass blank. They had a limited life and were hand made by a clever stagehand and were always in short supply and pricey. These very cloud designs were finally etched into aluminium by Rosco and Great American Market and became more available as well as affordable. I used clouds a lot."

In the late forties George Gill made a star cut-out and put it in a followspot for a television variety show – probably Sid Caesar's *Show of Shows*. He later made some stock patterns, for off-the-shelf supply for Kleigl, Century and Strong equipment.

Someone had the bright idea of using a pre-tooled set of metal radiator covers – see illustration – and using them as gobos. Joel Rubin has researched the Kleigl archive, which is being donated to the Theatre Library at Ohio State University, which shows the first Kleigl catalogue with these radiator designs dated at September 1960.

Kraft Music Hall 1966 Man of La Mancha in colour – hand cut patterns in Kleigl 3kW ellipsoidals – Bill Klages.

In the late 1950s, when Jules Fisher began lighting he had patterns made by Century Lighting; the actual cutting was sub-contracted to a metal cutter using a jeweller's saw on a copper substrate.

Danny Franks was one of the very early television lighting designers in the US, starting with ABC in New York in the early fifties and remembers making hand cut aluminium 'patterns' for Kleigl ellipsoidal spotlights.

We believe that sometime after professionally-made custom gobos were available, there remained a tradition of hand making gobos. Beverly Emmons recalls that Richard Nelson hand-made many, for the show *Sunday in the Park* in 1984.

Many of the early designs were 'break-ups', for the 'dappling' effect mentioned by Francis Reid, and the provenance of one design, 'Lashes', still in the Rosco catalogue, is pleasing – we quote Jules Fisher:

"On the original production of Jesus Christ Superstar in NYC (1971?) the audience entered the auditorium to see a vertical wall of stone instead of an act curtain. Projected in gobos were broken wiggly lines meant to look like cracks in the wall.

"When the overture began the lines became animated, a metaphor of the 'lashes' to come. To accomplish this, besides the hand-cut copper templates, I mounted an 18-inch clear acrylic wheel in front of each lens. The $1/8$ inch thick wheels had baked in my kitchen oven for about five minutes until they were irregularly warped. When they commenced to rotate on cue, the 'cracks' became animated 'lashes'. I am sure the metaphor was mainly in my mind."

Similarly we find in the UK that one of the designs from the DHA Lighting catalogue, Reflected Water 1, design no 903 (now part of the Rosco collection, 77903), originated from a holiday photo of the reflected pattern of light across the hull of a Greek fishing boat; whilst another design (DHA 913 Brush Strokes, now Rosco 77913) came about from the idle doodles of a staff member with a bottle of type-writer correction fluid!

Still other gobo designs came about as design requirements for particular shows: a five-part stained glass window each section of which was placed into five profiles and coloured with separate colour filters before being carefully aligned to produce a single, detailed multi-coloured image was made for David Hersey's design for the *Sound of Music*. This was deemed a novel technological development requiring precision etching and calculation of beam angles at the time.

Marvin Gelman (Lighting Services Inc.) told Jules Fisher of an experience from his days of live television in the late fifties when he was lighting a Sunday morning religious programme. He put a lace pattern paper doily in an ellipsoidal reflector spotlight aimed at a surface behind the programme's logo. On cue he turned on the spotlight and the audience saw the image for a second before it instantly burst into flame.

Kleigl and Century were marketing for television and certainly one of the prompts for the business was not creative – the plain set walls caused camera noise, and an image and shadow casts from a gobo minimised this.

In the late sixties, Paul Marantz, a class-mate to one David Hersey, was working in the R&D lab at Century and saw a photo-etching process for small parts for dimmer boards and had the idea of photo-etching custom gobo designs using this process on stainless steel.

Richard Broadhurst tells us: Custom made gobos, as we know them today, first appeared in the UK in the late 1960s, predominantly in television studios, with the BBC first employing those from the American company, Berkey Colortran.

In the late 1960s, Bill Millar, a lighting director at the BBC who mainly worked on light entertainment, started his own company, Miltel, producing etched metal stock and custom designs. Along with DHA Lighting these were the only companies manufacturing gobos in the UK.

Miltel was sold to R.B. Lighting (Richard Broadhurst) in the 1980s who subsequently sold the company to DHA Lighting. These original patterns can still be purchased today from Rosco.

In 1971 Jules Fisher and Paul Marantz started the partnership, Fisher Marantz Architectural Lighting Design.

Fisher suggested to Joe Tawil in the early 1970s that there should be an off-the-shelf collection of stainless steel patterns.

Fisher and other designers created 24 designs, which were made by Berkey Colortran whilst Joe Tawil formed GAM (Great American Market), and added another 36 designs.

In the early days, when GAM considered making a range of gobos, they found that there were many versions of the ellipsoidal spotlight and every manufacturer seemed to have their own pattern holder, if they had one at all. No two were the same, varying widths and depth. So they made a 4" wide x 5" deep pattern n 0.005" stainless steel which users could cut to required size with scissors. This enabled GAM to make one size of actual image. The DHA and Rosco

16 Patterns from radiator covers.

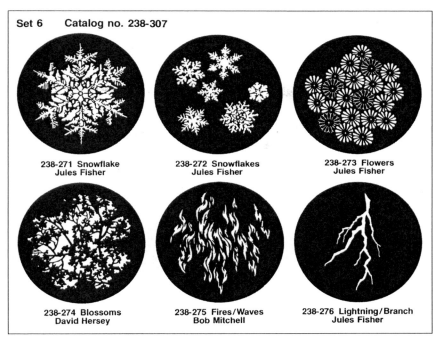

Set 6   Catalog no. 238-307

238-271 Snowflake
Jules Fisher

238-272 Snowflakes
Jules Fisher

238-273 Flowers
Jules Fisher

238-274 Blossoms
David Hersey

238-275 Fires/Waves
Bob Mitchell

238-276 Lightning/Branch
Jules Fisher

Some 1974 pattern designs – GAM 1974 catalogue.

approach was to create a series of sizes to optimise the projection area and provide holders for each fixture, with a series of zigzags on the bottom, to permit screwdriver access to adjust the alignment of the image.

The original Colortran collection was sold in 1980 to Stan Miller of Rosco Laboratories, who added it to the David Hersey range, which Rosco handled exclusively in the USA.

Authors' note: we asked lighting designer Francis Reid to recall his early gobo experiences for us and are pleased to reproduce his contribution unchanged here:

Early Gobo Experiences

Yesterday I opened my trunk of old lighting plans for what is probably the first time this century. No need to drown to see life flashing before you – just look at the rig plans of mostly forgotten shows!

During the winter of 1961/62, I heard (I think probably from June Dandridge, Glyndebourne's production manager) of some particularly good dappled light in a new production at Covent Garden. The show was over so I couldn't see it but I contacted Bill Bundy who explained how they had cut irregular holes in metal plates to put in profile gates.

Pelleas et Melisande was then in planning for the 1962 Glyndebourne summer season. Debussy's music is all about light and Beni Montresor's design used lots of gauze with the many forest scenes just crying out for dappled sunlight and moonlight. So we experimented with a bit of crude bashing, punching and cutting into

Francis Reid.

metal that happened to be around but was heavier than we really needed.

For the show, our main instruments for projecting "gobos" (we didn't know the word gobo and called them "dapples") were Strand Pattern 53s – the last 1kW profile to be based on a T2 lamp. There were four on each of the over-stage lighting bridges (one bridge immediately inside the proscenium and one midstage). These bridges and the OP (stage right) fly gallery (there was no fly gallery PS due to the theatre having initially been built too close to the house) were manned so that lighting could be re-gelled and refocused during the performances … and in this *Pelleas* it was done extensively. (The Number 1 bridge was focused by one of the gardeners who was just about the most sensitive focuser I ever worked with in my entire career; the Number 2 bridge by a blacksmith from the Glyndebourne estate forge). We also used some Pattern 23s. The whole evening was played behind a black gauze as a softener. For the musical interludes behind scenes, we projected on to this gauze from a Pani 2k (not enough space for a 5k) and dropped in a black to cover scene change and re-focus.

It was a critical hit, for example, the *Financial Times* review:

> *One of those serene evenings … the enchanted scenes behind the gauze begin to glow and to capture the imagination and emotions, as Vittorio*

Gui's conducting and Carl Ebert's production – both strong, but both sensitive – bring the drama to life. ...drenched with tonal and visual beauty and very clearly conceived. Maeterlinck's symbolism in every single scene is of light: the small areas within which we move and can apprehend some of the features of those near to us: the shadows of half-knowledge: the encircling darkness pierced occasionally by a ray like those from the great ship of the third scene. This literary symbolism is here most wonderfully realised in scenic terms too – and the name of the lighting director, Francis Reid, should be mentioned.

In my *Hearing the Light* memoirs I wrote about the production thus ...

I found myself no longer resisting the circumstances that seemed to be propelling me toward a career in lighting design and it was the 1962 summer season which established me. Carl Ebert returned to Glyndebourne for a final production. 'Pelleas et Melisande' is not my kind of opera but it would be several years before I realised that my work is much better when the music does not trigger too deep an emotional response in me. Beni Montressor filled the raked stage with gauzes of an impressionistic forest. Within this, significant environmental items such as the tower, well, and bed were set and struck behind a front gauze during the orchestral interludes. There was insufficient time during afternoon performance preparations to set each scene for focusing, so there had to be some extremely fast but delicately sensitive re-focusing by the crew during the short musical interludes. Jack the gardener tended his spotlights on the lighting bridge as if they were delicate blossoms.

During the winter, the grapevine had whispered that Bill Bundy at Covent Garden was using a simple way of giving light a dappled quality by inserting metal plates drilled with irregular holes into the gates of profile spotlights. This may have been the first use of break-up gobos: I had never seen or heard of the technique before and I am fairly certain that it was also unknown to Strand who were the major manufacturer of profile spots. Dappled light was ideal for the 'Pelleas' forest and the textured paint on the textured gauzes reacted beautifully to the textured light. This production was the start of a close collaboration with the scenic artist Charles Bravery. He taught me so much. I visited his paint frame and he came to my lighting rehearsals. I lit into his paint he painted into my light. I adjusted my filters and he modified his pigments.

Ebert preferred to draw out an interpretation from within his actors rather than superimpose it externally. The interpretation remained largely Ebert's own but his method ensured that the acting was so sincere that any hint of superficiality was rare in his productions. Ebert often employed a similar technique to stimulate his creative team. There was one particular moment during the lighting of 'Pelleas' when I had really lost my way. He knew what was wanted but, rather than tell me, he picked up his score from the production desk saying: "Come, Francis my dear, let us go for a walk in the forest." As we walked to and fro between the gauzes, he talked about Maeterlinck's poem and Debussy's musical response to its verbal imagery. He talked of the light in the text and the light in the score. By the time we reached the well at the front of the stage, I knew how it had to look. He could have told me. But he preferred to draw it out from within me.

The conductor was Vittorio Gui and on the night of the first performance the veteran maestro sat on his customary chair in the wings to await his call to go into the pit. One by one the singers approached him to pay their respects. Then he beckoned me over. "Francis, I worked with Debussy on the premiere of this opera. I know what he wanted and we are giving it to him tonight." It was his use of the word 'we' which particularly thrilled me.

A mention by Andrew Porter in the Financial Times *helped kick my lighting design career into orbit.*

I think that Theatre Projects (Richard Pilbrow or Robert Ornbo) used break-ups for the first time at Stratford during that summer.

The following summer Glyndebourne did a new *Magic Flute* for which textured light was essential. The basis of the design was eight periakti: three-sided columns just big enough to enclose radio-cued students who could glide and rotate them to move into magically new formations for each scene. Under break-up gobos, the scene changes were like a kaleidoscope. The first entrance of the Queen of the Night was magical. The periakti formed a perspective' V through which she travelled on a high castored rostrum down the centre line of the stage from its deepest point (about 60 feet). All her costume, with the exception of the corsage, was incorporated into the rostrum design and as she moved downstage, she was cross-lit with broken dappled light. Her arrival at the front of the stage coincided with her first note and a cross-fade to frontal light. Mozart provides a terrific entrance musically, and the challenge was met visually.

At this time, incidentally, thyristors and presetting were still two years away and memory but a dream – we were still working with a 1934

Siemens Bordoni plus two 10-way ADB autotransformer portables – and with four operators to be coordinated.

The Italian and German directors and designers working on the rest of these early 1960 seasons were intrigued – all looking up into the fly tower to expecting to see lots of film-studio style cuckoloris. Hardly surprising given the relative absence of profile spots from the then PC-dominated central Europe lighting practice.

We were still calling them 'dapples' at this time but discovering that we could use more workable metal – particularly discarded litho plates and freezing/cooking dishes.

Into this century, on my British Council teaching excursions into areas of the world with lesser theatre technology, I was still keeping the metal cover from my airline meal to demonstrate (with nail scissors) the break-up gobo principle (before going on to show Rosco break-up and silhouette examples followed by slides of sample catalogue pages).

In the early 1960s I soon found that gobo break-up was a wonderful assistance to the last act extended moonlight scenes that so many operas have. Breaking-up the moonlight enabled higher intensity levels without loss of atmosphere and modelling. On a revival of *The Marriage of Figaro* I applied this to a re-light of Oliver Messel's final garden scene with was hugely satisfying. (And as a light designer I rarely reached anything close to satisfaction!)

I am not sure when we learned to call them gobos. The first appearance of the word gobo (rather than dapple) on one of my plans is 1966. Interestingly it is spelt gobbo – which suggests that I had heard the word rather than seen it. However, I must have been using it since 1963 because the plan for Martin Walser's *The Rabbit Race* at the 1963 Edinburgh Festival shows "G" on Pattern 53s and 23s with Cinemoid 38 and 50 scattered through the rig in appropriate positions for dappling a set which had a big tree as its centrepiece. The venue was the temporary thrust stage (originally devised by Tyrone Guthrie) in the Church of Scotland Assembly Hall. This production showed me how useful gobos were on thrust stages; I subsequently used them regularly on open stages but it was not until the final years of my career that I had me a ball in a couple of Chichester pantomimes including lots of rotation and aisles lit as forest glades when used for actor entrances.

Certainly the word was established by 1969 when my *Anne of Green*

Gables (at the New Theatre, which became the Albery and is now the Gielgud) was dubbed *Anne of Green Gobos* by the crew. (During the get-out, one of the gobos was left in a front-of-house Pattern 23 and I'm told that Joe Davis coming in with the next show uttered quite a few colourful expletives about the lighting output of Strand luminaires before the offending gobo was discovered and extracted). These were still hand-made metal bashings made in the Donmar hire workshops.

And later in 1969 for *Lucky Peter's Journey* at the Coliseum, when I asked for 30 break-ups, Sadler's Wells (as ENO then was) asked for a design. I drew a few typical irregular holes on the back of an envelope to indicate rough shape and scale. They then commissioned John Roffey (ex-Sadlers Wells, then at Greenwich) to drill them out of thick metal, exactly to my drawing and all identical!

Through the sixties and into the early seventies, there was only one occasion when I used gobos other than random break-up. That was for the 1967 Glyndebourne production of *La Boheme* when I had long ridges cut to light snowdrift groundrows.

Long before gobo rotators, *Turn of the Screw* at Morley College in 1966 was my first attempt to get movement into a gobo. A pair of pattern 23/N with gobos had standard Strand colour wheels attached. The filter numbers are not on the plan but I remember them as three or four closely related early autumnal subtractives, distributed in a different randon sequence across the five slots on each instrument. The rotational speed was non-adjustable but miraculously it was just right for the rhythm of Britten's horse drawn coach. So we played the *Journey to Bly* prologue with the singer static and just the pair of 'moving' gobos. This production received fantastic notices (the *Times, Guardian, Financial Times* and *Opera Magazine* all went orgasmic about the lighting). For the critical response and the circumstances of the production see pages 62 and 63 in *Hearing the Light*.

I can't remember when I first used DHA /Rosco catalogue litho-gobos but I do remember that my first order for a gobo from artwork was in 1978 *The Great American Backstage Musical* at the Regent Theatre (an announcer/microphone line drawing).

Much of my use of gobos was always very out-of-focus – just to make a very slight texture in the light – and very often it would have taken a very experienced eye to realise that gobos were in use.

Because the key to texture is the superimposition of beams of differing hard/soft focus, subtly different filters and differing break-up pattern. I found the Pattern 23 to be very useful, right up, if I remember rightly, until my final panto in 2001. It was small, easy to soft focus, a 2kW dimmer could feed four and they were usually easy to find in theatre store-rooms when the rental budget was low.

Juko Sato
Lighting Designer, Japan: Theatre

Before 1982, Japanese lighting designers were using hand cut aluminium gobos, so it was a surprise when I went to the USA to study lighting design to see the stainless steel gobos at Great American Market and to see the early Vari*lite fixtures and the first glass gobos.

For me, there are two reasons to use gobos: to put an emotive accent to the three dimensional space and when the stage scenery does not specifically explain the 'space', which means there is a need to create this with lighting qualified by symbolism with gobos, usually custom-made.

Abigail Rosen Holmes

Lighting and Video Designer, USA:
Concert, Television, and Special Events

I use gobos to produce lighting which is intentionally uneven and imperfect to bring a sense of the organic into our artificially created environments.

In the air I use gobos to create architecture out of light and smoke – extending and redefining space outside the restrictions of the conventional stage.

I have designed a lot of custom gobos for automated fixtures. I can picture exactly how I want the gobo to work, and I like creating original elements which become part of the design. Maybe it is an extension of my background as an art major.

There are over 2000 custom gobos in my garage for discontinued fixtures. Maybe I'll make them into windchimes one day when I retire!

DEVELOPMENT AND MANUFACTURE

Ben M Rogers

Lighting and Video Designer, UK and Cyprus: Live Events, Theatre, Concerts, Product Launches, Conferences, Festivals.

For me the gobo is the most effective and dynamic way to add texture to the performance space. It gives the opportunity to not only sculpt the set with light, but also the air itself, adding a tangible further dimension to the scenic image. Whilst I will often utilise the pictorial nature of a window or similar pattern, it is the abstract gobos – from soft textures through to glass patterns and colourisers – that I find most interesting in creating further character and dimension to even the most simple of sets.

I see the implementation of lighting in theatre as equivalent to the role of a cinematographer in film: it is the art by which we can direct the attention of the audience as we wish. In many respects it is the absence of light on a stage that can be more visually stimulating than a brightly lit space – the use of gobos is a key factor in this. Similarly, there is some truth on the term 'fixing it with light' as an appreciation of the potential that crafted lighting has to change, morph and animate the stage picture.

3 METAL GOBOS

Gobos can be manufactured from metal or glass and we will be looking at both in more detail in the next few chapters, starting here with metal.

Metal Gobo Manufacture

There are two ways of manufacturing metal gobos. Chemical etching, and more recently laser etching.

The process for chemical etching breaks down into six main steps as follows:

Standard metal gobo.

- Design advice and artwork processing
- Production of graphic film tool
- Metal preparation
- Printing and developing
- Chemical etching
- Stripping and removing of gobos from metal sheet

Artwork

The customer's design is adapted as necessary, then sized and placed into a gobo template in a suitable graphics computer program. Metal gobos require 'tags' to hold the design together, much like a stencil, and complex designs may be simplified for smaller sizes of gobo.

Whilst it is possible to redraw faxes and low resolution jpegs, the best formats for artwork for metal gobos are Illustrator vector eps, or high resolution Photoshop documents.

Production Of Graphic Film Tool

Computer software is used to step and repeat the gobos across a page to enable the etching of a number of gobos at one time.

This sheet of artwork is then laser plotted to create a film 'tool'. Two black and clear films are prepared; one for each side of the metal which allows etching from both sides. This enables 'half etch' detail to be etched from one side, such as a company logo and gobo number.

Metal Preparation
Gobos are usually manufactured from 0.1 - 0.2mm stainless steel. Some companies use black steel which is advantageous due to its low reflectivity (i.e. less flare within the lantern optics) and durability. The metal sheet is cleaned and cut, then coated with photosensitive resist on both sides.

Printing and Developing
The coated metal sheet is placed between the two films of the tool and exposed to UV light on both sides to transfer the image onto the metal.

The areas which are protected from the UV light by the graphic film tool remain soft. The sheet of metal is then chemically developed away, leaving the exposed metal ready for etching.

Chemical Etching
The metal sheet is passed through the etching machine where a sprayed acidic solution removes the exposed metal.

Stripping and Removal of Gobos From Metal Sheet
Any resist coating remaining is stripped from the metal, and each gobo is broken out of the sheet, inspected and packed.

Metal Gobo Materials
Metal gobos have been, and are, etched on a variety of different metals.

Stainless Steel
Hardrolled stainless steel is by far the most popular material with thicknesses varying from 0.005" to 0.008" depending on manufacturer. It is durable under heat and takes design detail well. Generally speaking, the thicker the metal, the more hard wearing the gobo. Manufacturers may argue the merits of thinner metal taking finer detail against the extra heat resilience of the thicker metal and corresponding extra time (and

cost) it takes to etch, but there is equal validity in all these arguments and stainless steel still remains the most useful of etching materials.

Brass alloy
Less common is brass alloy which claims to have thermal characteristics that help reduce heat distortion and burning.

Nickel Silver
Nickel Silver is a slightly softer than stainless steel and very easy to etch. It may not have quite the same durability of stainless steel but is often offered as an economical alternative for shorter term installations.

Phosphor Bronze
Phosphor Bronze was at one time a very popular material for mass production since it offered an economical yet heat resistant option for OEM gobos in moving head fixtures. However, long term degradation set in as lamp temperatures increased and the material eventually fell out of favour.

Aluminium
Aluminium is not able to render the fine detail of stainless steel gobos but, despite having a lower melting point than steel, its looser molecular structure makes it more malleable and less inclined to permanent damage under intense heat. It therefore retains the integrity of the gobo design and is popular for OEM gobo production within moving head fixtures where light output and uniformity of design is of paramount importance.

Black Coated Gobos
One manufacturer, Goboland, has succeeded in developing a 'black' steel gobo which has a non-reflective, heat-resistant black coating on both sides. This goes a considerable way towards cutting down on

Goboland Black Steel Gobo.

internal reflection and the result is a much clearer image with less 'halo' and minimal loss of light. The concept was given a PLASA Award for Innovation in 2008.

OEM (Original Equipment Manufacture) Production

The manufacture of OEM gobos – sets of gobos which are shipped within manufacturers' moving head fixtures – requires an additional level of expertise in the manufacturing process.

Precise, consistent control over sizing and image quality is imperative if all fixtures are to maintain a continuity of image across all units, regardless of which production batch they derive from. This is a very important quality when using multiple units in a production or for rental houses wishing to maintain parity within their hire stock.

An increase in light output requirements for moving lights brought about a corresponding increase in gobo size. This, along with improved cooling technology and increasing optical efficiency allowed (and necessitated) the use of aluminium where the larger gobo size enabled the use of greater design detail than was possible with earlier smaller gobos.

Any buckling of the aluminium in the heat of the lantern is reversed once the gobo cools so the designs are more durable and less distorted when projected. This also makes it more likely that each gobo design in each unit will match those in other units, even after repeated use.

However, aluminium is notoriously difficult to etch since its reaction to the acid etchant creates an exothermic reaction within the metal, creating its own heat which speeds up the rate of etching. This makes the etching rate very erratic and difficult to control.

An 'open' image, i.e. one that lets more light through during projection, will etch more quickly than a

MAC 500 aluminium gobo wheel.

'closed' one. Similarly, open areas and closed areas within a single gobo design are also subject to the same disparate etch rates.

This becomes particularly complicated when multiple images are being etched at the same time, for example on a MAC500 wheel. This calls for a fine balancing act to ensure the 'closed' images are etched enough without the 'open' images being over etched or even destroyed. Any gobo design destined for etching on aluminium therefore has to be micro-modified almost beyond recognition to be successfully etched by the gobo manufacturer. DHA Lighting worked extensively with Martin Professional in developing a successful means of acid etching gobos from aluminium in a process perfected by trial, error and experience.

Max Keller
Lighting Designer, Lecturer and Writer, Germany: Theatre,

The brighter the light, the deeper the shadow. We make a point that, from spotlights with a projection plane, the light shines into the dark as clean and clear as possible.

Gobos offer alternatives to separate the light beam in different light/dark zones, in logical and fantasy themes. As always in technology, innovations explode sometimes fast, sometimes slow, but they do happen. Static gobos made of thin steel, glass gobos with colour themes, rotating and moveable themes; this is today's standard.

Applied individually they are always an "eye-catcher". But this does not mean one should deploy these sophisticated theme projections continuously. A clever mix of different light types is always the better way.

For my light designs, which I support with gobo technology themes, I almost always choose structure themes, refracting the light irregularly and fuzzy.

Fortunately, there are no rules for a decision; the only yardstick is the vision.

Aluminium is still used in OEM work but, with the improvements in glass technology and heat management systems, there is also widespread use of glass gobos – both imaged and textured – in OEM production.

Laser Etching

Laser etching of both metal and glass gobos has also been employed by manufacturers including Vari-lite, Rosco, DHA and Apollo Design Technology.

The basic steps to laser cutting gobo images are as follows:

- Design artwork is processed
- Digital information of the design is fed to the laser
- Laser shop inspects art program for possible mistakes/corrections
- Laser entry point cuts are added to the artwork and it is saved to a queue
- Metal is loaded in the laser and the program pulled up

The gobo is then processed by cutting, or ablating, the outline of the image until the metal drops away.

There is some discussion as to the relative merits or disadvantages of this form of gobo production, but it is now established as an alternative commercial manufacturing process to acid etching.

Advantages:

- no films or photo resist layer
- no chemicals
- clean and sustainable for glass production

Disadvantages:

- requires immense amount of power, especially when etching metal, which may affect green credentials
- comparatively slow
- does not radically improve accuracy or fine line facility over acid etching on metal

4 METAL ARTWORK DEVELOPMENTS

It is not just etching procedures which determine the quality of the finished result. Artwork and methods of artwork preparation are of equal importance and much research and development has gone, and continues to go, into perfecting this stage of the gobo making process. As lantern optics have improved and designers' creativity demands more choice, so the need for better quality products increases.

Lighting designer David Hersey remembers: "The first gobos we used were pieces of aluminium with holes punched in them using a screwdriver!" Things have moved on considerably since then with Hersey realising that printed circuit technology could be applied to acid etching of steel gobos.

"Our initial attempt to etch an IBM logo was disastrous. We tried to do it in the kitchen sink but discovered we were using acid proof steel – the gobo remained unetched while the acid totally destroyed the sink! After further trials we eventually succeeded!"

David Hersey Associates, founded in 1971, initially concentrated on custom designs but, by 2004, had developed the largest catalogue range of over 1200 stock designs. This range has now been absorbed into the Rosco catalogue after DHA Lighting, as it became, was acquired by Rosco in 2005.

In 1979 David brought Wyatt Enever into the business, whom he had met via Dawson Strange Photography. As a photographer with qualifications in printing technology and photographic reproduction, and with a background in cartography and chemical etching at the Ministry of Defence, Enever was to bring significant advancements to gobo artwork and production. The following have been the most influential in modernising and refining current production techniques within the gobo industry.

Double Sided Etching
Single sided etching (i.e. only one side of the metal is coated by a photo-resist layer) gives razor sharp edges that make handling hazardous and gave imprecise definition of the image. Double sided etching – where

a second photo resist film is placed on the obverse side of the metal sheet with an identical mirror image of the design to be etched – allows the acid to attack the metal from both sides giving the design less room to spread.

This allows greater control and accuracy and results in finer designs. This opened up a whole new area for making corporate logos in addition to finer images and subtler 'break-ups'. It also enables 'half-etching' where information such as the gobo name, catalogue number and even a bar code can be etched into one side of the gobo as a useful identification tool.

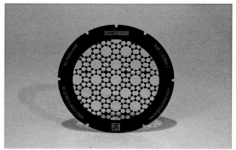

Double sided etching allows much finer designs to be produced.

Pin Holes

Double sided etching dramatically reduces the number of 'pinholes', specks of light caused by dust particles on the film, so reducing the number of rejected gobos in the process.

Registration

Double sided etching demands absolute precision to achieve perfect registration of the film tool. Image registration techniques from the mapping industry uses a pin registration system to maintain alignment between several layers of images. Enever was able to transpose this technique into the registration of gobo film tools.

Mesh/Half-Tone

Half-tone imaging is a technique which produces an image with subtle grey-scale tones instead of just 'black' or 'white'. This makes possible more realistic images, such as clouds, and dispenses with 'tagging' (see page 53) to give finer detail. A greyscale image is translated into a bitmap of coarse dots in Photoshop and hung on a crossline fine mesh which, when projected slightly off-focus, is barely distinguishable against the main image.

"It may sound a bit crude now," continues Wyatt, "but projecting a metal gobo with a tonal image was a big innovation."

A similar artwork technique was then employed for glass gobos. Here, instead of using a conventional registration screen, Enever used a series of random dots (now called 'diffusion dither' in Photoshop and subsequently introduced into Agfa filmsetters) to create the tonal image. "To the best of my knowledge, no-one had done this before," says Enever, "and it turned out to be probably the biggest development in gobo quality of all." This, along with the greater resolution capabilities of glass, mean that mesh gobos have been largely superseded by glass.

Meshed or half tone imaging for more subtle grey scale tones and finer detail.

Keystoning

Keystoning is the manipulation of an image to counteract the frequent case when a projector or lantern cannot be rigged 'square on' to the projection surface. A gobo with a pre-distorted image can be created so that it will project 'true' when the projector is hung in the predetermined position. The designer just needs to supply the gobo manufacturer with the size of image required, the make, model and focal length of the lantern and its precise position in relation to the projection surface (distance, height and offset) for the keystone calculation to be made.

Enever was not the first to create a pre-distorted image since Dawson Strange Photography had been calculating single plane distortions with Robert Ornbo – another designer from Richard Pilbrow's Theatre Projects – mainly for slides. It was DSP that first showed Enever the simple formula for a single plane distortion. Enever then decided that a double plane distortion had to be possible and set about calculating how it could be done. "I lost a few brain cells that weekend but just had to work it through," he says. "I worked it out long-hand and the maths were quite extraordinary!" Following this massive cerebral workout, DHA Lighting developed a keystone 'plug-in' for Adobe Illustrator which is still used to this day.

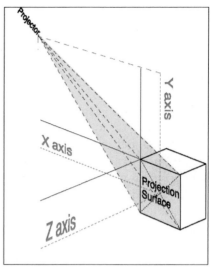

Predistortion of images can be calculated from distance, height and offset details of the projector.

Image projection before and after keystone correction.

Mike Le Fevre

Lighting Designer, UK:
Television. Treasurer and
Vice-Chair of Society
of Television Lighting
Designers.

My first ever, appallingly bad use of gobos, was for my school's 6th Form cabaret review in 1979. I remember the eager anticipation of flicking through the catalogue, the purchase order from the bursar, the collection of the package from the staff room, the "Just what are you up to boy?", the burnt fingers focusing…

The gobo was Rosco 77769 Ritz with a homemade colour wheel on the front of a Strand Patt 23, used as a straight projection on the back drop for the entire show! Ah! – the joys of ignorance, how little did I know … 27 years of lighting later I should now know better …

Nowadays my personal favourites are Reflected Water (Rosco 77903), Tie Dye (Rosco 77582), Ocelot (Medium) (Rosco 77409), Brush Stroke #2 (Rosco 77535) and *Les Mis* Grill #2 (Rosco 77978) which I hope I use with more subtlety and invention than my 16 year old self!

Light is the very essence of the universe; our ability to texture its beam, and that beam's interrelation to surface, gives so much more emotion, depth and 'feel' to our images. I encourage all to experiment and play, to understand the effects you can achieve and that of the underlying emotional response. Let your imagination rip!

And, yes, I did shine light through cellophane sweet wrappers in my childhood!

Hugh Chinnick
Lighting Designer, Hong Kong:
Architectural, Corporate, Exhibition.

In designing the lighting for the Hong Kong Maritime Museum, I wanted to include as much visual stimulation as possible and appropriate. Coming from a theatrical background, this obviously included projecting gobos onto the floor.

Gobos emulating a rotating compass, typhoon signal and GPS screen were easy, but when it came to a realistic radar screen, things got a little more tricky! How could I get the fading of the radar image as the sweep moves round, and have both static and moving images in the correct focus?

Fortunately, the sweep on a radar screen is very slightly soft, so using two gobos in different planes would work ... in theory. However, the radar screen artwork was quite detailed, so I chose a Derksen 100W tungsten projector rather than a theatrical unit, and experimented with a gobo rotator. Firstly a 'static' screen gobo was mounted in the Derksen's gobo slot. Then we produced artwork for the second 'sweep' gobo in Adobe

Illustrator using radial greyscale and a little cutting, masking and general experimentation! By mounting the 'sweep' gobo in the gobo rotator, the position of which can be adjusted in relation to the static gobo, we found that the theory worked. We had successfully created a fully functioning radar gobo which caught the eye of visitors, whilst the kids loved chasing the sweep."

5 GLASS GOBOS

Glass Gobos: An Introduction

Metal gobos have served the industry well and continue to do so, but with the development of glass gobo technology, we can summarise their merits and disadvantages.

Merits

- Inexpensive to manufacture
- Ease of volume production
- Metal is highly heat resistant
- Choice of metal type and finish
- Ease of making multiple gobo wheels for automated lights
- Thousands of 'standard' images from manufacturers around the world
- Ease of making low cost custom designs – quickly

Disadvantages

- No colour possible
- Need for 'tagging' for design support
- Although a fine mesh gives half tone images, the resolution is poor
- Increased availability of high quality image projectors like Selecon from Philips, ETC Source Four and the EDLT (Enhanced Definition Lens Tube), Robert Juliat SX profiles and the Dedolight range, means that there is a need for higher quality gobos
- Many automated lights call for very small diameter gobos, which make metal gobos and fine detail inadequate

The rapid development of glass gobo technology matches the improvement of image quality projection. We have a new set of design parameters, and new needs:

Glass gobos must provide:

- Stable heat resistant glass substrate
- Capability of withstanding high temperatures, without deformation, and capable of extreme thermal shock without cracking
- Ability to make single or multiple colour, and photographic quality images

- For colour gobos, the colour must withstand high temperatures, with no fading in life, or melting or separating from the substrate
- A good black is hard to achieve: 'black' areas must completely block light transmission and with no pin-holes
- Colour consistency
- Ease of making custom designs – relatively quickly

Glass Gobo Manufacture

This is a continually changing and improving technology; we set out an overview of the processes involved in the manufacture:

Principles

There are two ways of making glass gobos, Wet Etching and Laser Etching. These are not exhaustive accounts, but give some insight into the challenges and choices faced by gobo makers.

Full colour glass gobo illustrating the subtle colour tones achievable.

Wet Etching – Black and White

A Black and White glass gobo is like a very thin metal gobo, so thin that the lines need the support of a glass substrate. With that glass substrate, there is no need for 'tag' supports.

The process breaks down to 7 main steps:

- Artwork processing
- Mask output
- Exposing the material

Intricate detail on Black/White glass gobo: Four Horsemen of the Apocalypse.

- Developing
- Etching
- Cutting
- Quality Control

We can overview these steps:

Artwork – is converted to the best format for the image, sized and placed in a template

Mask Output – an image-setter is used to output a black and clear film used as a mask during the next stage

Exposing the material – the raw material is glass with an opaque metal coating on one side and a layer of photo-resist coating on top. The mask is placed on top and is exposed to ultra-violet (UV) light for a controlled time. The clear areas of the film allow the UV to pass to the photo-resist layer

Developing – the piece is placed in a developing solution, which dissolves the photo-resist where it was exposed to the UV

Etching – after rinsing, the piece is placed in an etch solution, which dissolves the metal coating

Cutting – the gobos are cut to size from the sheet of glass

Quality Control – the finished gobos are checked for pinholes and image quality

Wet Etching – Colour

Colour gobos consist of multiple gobos superimposed on each other. Typically, for full colour, these would be Cyan, Magenta, Yellow and Black (known as CMYK, where 'K' equals 'Black', or four colour process).

The manufacture is then similar to Black and White, using the colour separation software within the image-setter.

The dichroic colour coating

Full colour glass gobo.

on each layer is resistant to most acid etchants so specialised acids are used.

Assembly of the layers is performed under high magnification to ensure good registration of the separate image layers.

Laser Vapourising – Colour
Vapourising is known as 'ablation' and was pioneered in the 1990s.
The advantages are:
- No film output masks needed
- The image is cut directly on the glass
- Use of hazardous chemicals eliminated

The disadvantages are:
- Image resolution is not as high as the wet etch system.

The Future
Changes and improvements happen all the time, and the image quality will continue to improve – exciting times ahead!

Rosco and Glass Gobos
Rosco Laboratories in the US set up a plant in Austin Texas in 1994 specifically to make coloured dichroic glass and to develop glass gobos, all under one roof. Rosco also make metal and glass gobos in their London, England plant and, most recently, Paris.

In 1995 Rosco started etching colour glass gobos. Originally colour glass gobos had been made using straight etched dichroic colour but with no halftones. This was introduced with a set of 12 colours with Cyan, Magenta, Yellow, Black (K) mixing.

Conventional etchant chemicals tended to be toxic and undesirable to work with, and presented concerns for the environment. Subsequent research on etchants has resulted in better recycling and less chemical waste.

Electronic transmission of artwork simplified life for creating camera-ready artwork and cut down lead-time, making same day production practical and near normal. The long lead times in making full colour glass gobos have been continuously reduced – encouraged by the demands of end users – and technically it is possible to produce in one day or less.

Early full colour glass gobos were made up of four coloured layers,

Early full colour glass gobos could be up to 5.2mm thick. More recent versions like this 2.2mm version are much thinner, with some CYMK gobos little more than 1mm thick.

each of which was 1.1mm thick. This resulted in a 'sandwich' nearly 5mm thick in which it was impossible to focus all layers simultaneously. At the time of writing this has drastically reduced.

It is possible to make a full colour gobo on one layer of glass – a process which has been patented by Disney, but is not often used.

Rosco also took steps to improve the resolution of coloured glass gobos by adopting stochastic screening methods.

Stochastic screening is a technique that uses a random dot pattern, unlike conventional screening which uses a regular pattern of dots in straight rows.

Although conventional screening is effective for many images, stochastic screening is a much better choice for others. It works best for small images showing fine, angular lines, smooth reflective surfaces and graduated tones.

Conventional Screening
20% tint at 20x magnification

Stochastic Screening
20% tint at 20x magnification

Stochastic screening improves image quality by using a random dot pattern instead of conventional regular dots in straight rows.

With stochastic screening, images are reproduced with no moirés, rosettes or other effects. In short you get finer detail and truer colour. This is especially valuable in small images, like those needed for the Martin MAC 250.

Apollo Design Technology and Glass Gobos

At its outset in the early nineties, Apollo Design Technology concentrated only on custom gobos, manufactured on 8mm stainless steel, before starting to build up a stock of standard gobos.

By around 1997, CEO Joel Nichols began experimenting with the etching of glass gobos. First attempts in monochrome imaging used chrome coated glass capable of resolutions of 72dpi.

By the time of LDI 1999, glass gobo manufacturers were producing solid colour glass gobos and three-colour glass gobos were just coming on to the market in the form of three pieces of glass stuck together.

Apollo Design Technology dedicated its resources to create a process which could produce half tone colour-mix gobos, which it succeeded in doing within 4-6 months and the Apollo Design Color Scenic range of gobos was born.

Nichols also explored the possibilities of laser etching and, by 2006, felt his samples on both metal and glass gobos were good enough for Apollo to consider laser etching for custom and standard gobo production.

Between 2005-2008 Apollo Design Technology slowly started the transition from chemical etching to laser etching, completing the transition six months ahead of schedule without, claims Nichols, the customers or the industry at large spotting the difference.

Other Key Gobo Manufacturers

We mention here some other key gobo manufacturers who play significant roles in the development and production of gobos, although this is not an exhaustive world list by any means:

Great American Market

Great American Market (GAM Products, Inc) is a long established gobo maker in operation since the 1960s, with a large range of steel gobos in a selection of sizes, plus accessories and other motion effects.

Goboland

Goboland is a small, very experienced group of people who offer a wide range of steel and glass gobos, and have advanced skills for custom work and projection correction solutions.

Projected Image

Projected Image was established in 1999. They are associated with the Beacon group (see page 74) and provide a full catalogue of steel gobos, black and white glass and full CMYK coloured glass. A full custom service is also available.

Beacon AB

Beacon AB give material and technical support to an association of gobo producers which manufacture metal and glass gobos around the world. Their technology is associated with the production of CYMK glass gobos using very thin layers of glass upon a supporting glass substrate.

Mark Jonathan
Lighting Designer: Theatre, Opera, Dance, Ballet, Arena.

I remember when we didn't have gobos apart from some very basic break-ups. When we needed a gobo we used to cut them by hand in litho plate. Although I preferred to buy a pie, eat it and then use the tray for my gobo!

The advance in gobo technology went alongside the improvement in spotlights and their ability to be focused to a wider angle and be more visible. While using a gobo may not always be essential, I enjoy the possibilities they give me in being able to make an interesting texture in light, aiding the atmosphere and often giving me a base to disguise the light that might be there to illuminate the action.

Sometimes, I also find that I pluck out a gobo and use it in a different way with some surprising and original results.

Jackie Staines
*Former Chief Technician
and Lighting Designer,
Stephen Joseph Theatre in
the Round, Scarborough.*

Gobos were used
extensively at the Stephen
Joseph Theatre, both in the
classic texturing way by
using breakups and windows, and in a far
more literal way with symbols and patterns
projected onto the floor as 'scenery' for
highly stylised shows that had little or no
conventional scenery.

Ironically, the shows that had the greatest
need for this very unreal style of lighting
often also had the smallest budget,
so despite relying heavily on the need
for gobo projection, most had to be
designed and made for purpose – so out
came the litho plate and Stanley knives.

Breakups are pretty easy to achieve,
especially if they are going to be very soft
focused, but sometimes quite intricate
designs were required. They take time,
patience and skill, but can be achieved
if you have that time patience and skill –
and a lot of knife blades and plasters!

I started 'messing with lights' at the age of 12 in my local amateur
theatre and was soon crafting patterns from tinfoil – a Patt 23 with
a T1 doesn't get too hot. Stronger material is required for the heat
generated by TH lamps and condenser optics. And make sure the
field adjustment is flat otherwise your precious design will burn in
seconds.

6 MOVING LIGHTS AND GOBOS – A BRIEF HISTORY

Vari-Lite

The first moving light with gobos was developed in 1981 by three sound engineers – not lighting people. This first practical robotic stage lighting system was patented in July 1983 for the company Showco of Dallas, Texas.

We are delighted that Jim Bornhorst, one of those engineers, now Chief Scientist for PRG Lighting, gave us a detailed history of this development:

The VL1, as it was called, had four overlapping internal wheels, three of which held round dichroic filters for colour changing and the fourth, varying diameter holes to control the projected beam diameter.

In the final design six round apertures were used to control the beam size and two gobo patterns were added: an elongated rectangle resembling a laser line that could be moved using the pan and tilt, and an arrangement of 16 small holes which became affectionately known as 'The Bathtub Drain'. Especially effective in fog, this projected as an expanding beam shower which could be rotated and swept about the stage like a giant bristle brush.

In 1984 work began on Series 200, the next generation of moving light with many mechanical, electrical and optical improvements. VL1 aluminium gobos had deteriorated rapidly in the intense arc light so Vari-lite developed highly reflective multi-layer coatings for glass gobos in the Series 200 using a photolithographic process to selectively etch away the coating. One of the most successful glass patterns was a simple circle which projected as a cone of light which emulated the cone formed when a laser is quickly scanned in a circle.

The VL2 had 16 trapezoidal glass gobos clustered around the circumference of a wheel hub attached to the shaft of a stepper motor and cemented to T-shaped metal holders which made them easily interchangeable.

Internally reflected light was a problem so a special coating was devised as a multi-layer absorber or 'dark mirror' which absorbed any back-reflected light and resulted in an image with very high contrast.

In 1992 Vari-lite developed a method of vapourising (ablating) the glass gobos' optical coating in a pattern, allowing rapid manufacture of gobos from electronic artwork files.

In March 1998 a US Patent was issued covering a system to write vector images and bit-mapped photorealistic images. A couple of the first remarkable images were that of Albert Einstein and the Taj Mahal.

Work in the early 2000s focused on the development of durable colour images that could withstand the intense heat of 1200W lamps. Two processes emerged:

The Beacon process used three sheets of ultra thin glass, each coated with a dichroic filter of one of the three subtractive colours. The coated microsheets were photoetched with the appropriate colour-separated gobo pattern and a fourth backing layer added containing the black and white information.

Reproduction of Vari-lite's early glass gobos: Albert Einstein and the Taj Mahal.

The drawback to this multi-layered process was that fast projection lenses in moving lights could not resolve all four layers sharply so the image often needed to be in soft focus.

In the late 'nineties and early 2000s Vari-Lite developed a monolithic coloured gobo process where all the colour layers lay essentially in the same plane having been sequentially deposited and etched on the same piece of glass. This was based on a Disney patent which Vari-Lite licensed.

The gobos were able to resolve detail in the image at the five micron level and withstand the thermal radiation of a 1200W lamp. Jules Fisher used the process extensively for his Tony Award winning presentation of *Jane Eyre* on Broadway.

High End Systems

Another US company which helped pioneer the introduction of glass gobos was High End Systems.

One requirement of their research was to leverage the in-house dichroic coated glass manufacture, which would allow them to make gobos in colour and, of less importance to them at the time, to allow the use of disconnected and more detailed patterns than were possible with steel.

The photolithography research took two years, with the goal of moving all products to glass.

As time went on and after many, many etching experiments and trials with in-house staff and lighting design practitioners more and more importance was put on the use of detailed grey scale patterns and the use of colour diminished somewhat. The economics of colour were also a contributory factor.

The first black and white 'lithos' were used in a trade show in 1992, in an Intellabeam fixture.

What became clear was that the three dimensional quality possible from a grey scale or detailed patterned monochrome glass gobo could produce a stunning effect, particularly when added to the dynamics of beam movement and gobo rotation. It was also apparent that too many colour gobos could be limiting to the lighting designer who didn't want the fixture dictating his colour choice. Far better to use black/white and allow the lighting designer to pick the colours.

At the same time coloured custom patterns were selling well. However, a large number of these were for commercial use in product launches and so very often featured a corporate or product logo. This may have been a great use of the technology but was not the kind of thing that could be used in the standard shipping product.

Mike Wood remembers many meetings with the development team and the artistic staff where they had dozens, if not hundreds, of pattern designs from the graphic artists spread out on the table and from which they tried to pick a standard set of patterns for the Cyberlight models. Slightly arcane lists of rules were made up as to what they wanted; for example, every fixture must have a 'tunnel' gobo for that laser tunnel effect but it didn't have to be round. They also looked for patterns that could serve dual roles – perhaps a pattern that gave a good aerial effect when hard focused but was also usable as a break up pattern on scenery when slightly softened or run through a break up glass. They also wanted a brand similarity between the various models that kept the High End style but also made each model unique.

Last but not least the patterns had to be manufacturable to a consistency level that meant that a gobo made today would match one made two years ago. This was a real driver to the standardisation and automation of the litho etching process. An LD doesn't want to bring up a bank of 12 luminaires he has hired from a rental company (that were perhaps purchased and manufactured years apart) and see 12 different versions of the same pattern. Just as an LD expected colours to match across fixtures, High End felt the patterns must match as well. Greyscale patterns with very small dot shading were particularly difficult to manufacture consistently but were so important to the concept that manufacturing had to improve to allow their use in the standard product. This was a key reason for delaying full conversion to glass patterns until 1995, even though custom patterns had been in production for a number of years. The manufacturing capability to make all the patterns look the same, every day, every week, every year had to be in place first.

The final selection for the first Cyberlight wheel illustrates the selection reasoning:

The Laser Tunnel 'effects' (5) which, although simple, works so well in a glass gobo – no supporting wires. Shimmering stars (3) works as both an aerial and as a break up as does (6) Egyptian Space. Egyptian Space also contains detailed 3D shading so adds a new effect to the LD's arsenal when projected and is particularly effective when backed by changing colours. (4) Psy-Dye was a full colour pattern that showed the capabilities of the process but the cost and deliberate limiting of colour for the reasons stated above meant that one was enough. Conoid (7) was also a triple purpose aerial/break up/3D shaded pattern which left two slots (2) Alien Star and (8) Disconnect as high resolution projection imagery.

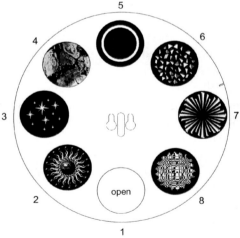

Gobo selection for the first High End Cyberlight static wheel.

Martin Professional

Martin Professional A/S, based in Denmark was the first European company in the moving light industry to emerge as a world player.

Martin Professional first started to use gobos in scanners and disco lighting in the late eighties, with much experimentation in materials, shapes and sizes.

The earliest was the RoboScan 804, which had a wedge shaped gobo flag of phosphor bronze, with three etched gobo designs and an 8mm open area. The flag offered a choice of different gobo designs to the lighting designer but these had to be changed manually in a time consuming process which involved opening up the fixture.

A step forward was made with the RoboScan 805 which offered three designs and an open aperture on an automated gobo wheel which changed on a rotating axis.

Throughout the progress of the RoboScan range, the choice of gobo material changed from phosphor bronze to stainless steel for durability and then to aluminium: so although the gobos became more rugged, they also lost definition.

Martin RoboScan 804 showing phosphor bronze gobo 'flag'.

The highly successful PAL 1200 and PAL 1200FX scanners included both stainless steel gobos, and structured and textured monochrome glass gobos.

Martin PAL 1200 FX module with static and rotating gobos of metal, dichroic and textured glass.

Most gobos at this time were outsourced: the metal to DHA in London and the colours from OCLI. Later Rosco and Beacon were to come on board with coloured images.

In the late nineties the MAC 250 and the MiniMAC moving heads were the first in the Martin range to have single colour dichroic gobos which were etched in-house before being cut to size with a water cutter.

However, the MAC 500 was perhaps the biggest jump forward in gobo design offering a full 360° aluminium gobo wheel with nine gobo designs and an open aperture. It also had a rotating gobo wheel consisting of five individually rotating and indexable gobos. The fixed wheel was later to be superseded by a slotted system where single 28mm gobos could be swapped out for alternative designs as required. The MAC 500 was supplied with a standard set of gobos and a replacement set of alternative designs.

The move from phosphor bronze to aluminium was determined by several factors. Intense heat easily distorted phosphor bronze and stainless steel. Although aluminium has a lower melting temperature than steel, it is more malleable and rugged, although notoriously difficult to etch. As light output requirements increased, so gobo size increased too. The larger gobo size enabled the use of aluminium which could hold more detail in a larger image size than was possible with previous, smaller images. Temperature issues improved as Martin got better at cooling technology.

Design consideration is also a critical factor in the success of a fixture and one in which Martin Professional has invested much time. Rental houses especially rely on consistency of image across models and find changing them to be too time consuming and costly in man-hours.

Martin Professional commissioned lighting designer Patrick Woodroffe, to create a range of designs for the new MAC 2000 Profile, its first all-glass gobo fixture, with a 30mm diameter image area. It was also the first to carry a two-colour glass gobo: one cyan and one magenta gobo sandwiched together.

As a follow on from this, a great amount of R&D was put into the design selection for the next Martin moving heads, the MAC 700 Profile, smartMAC and MAC 575, which was launched with a user-friendly combination of mid-air effects, textures and breakups. With a market spread across club venues, architecture and theatre, this can be a particularly complex process.

Lighting designers and users have keen regard for gobo designs. "Fixture popularity and versatility can be hugely dependent on gobos and we are very aware that they are a critical feature," states Martin Professional's Simon Allan, "We have to think not just about the design, but how they will be used, how positioned, how they will look when used in haze, from the side, rotating, in combination or with colour. Every aspect is considered and each aspect plays a vital part in the light's success."

Later fixtures from Martin Professional include those of the Performance range which are designed primarily for theatre use and carry a miniature animation wheel. This interacts with a gobo image to create movement and the illusion of water ripples, fire effects or clouds.

Patrick Woodroffe gobo collection for MAC 2000.

Ken Billington
Lighting Designer, USA: Musicals, Opera, Spectaculars, Theme and Architecture.

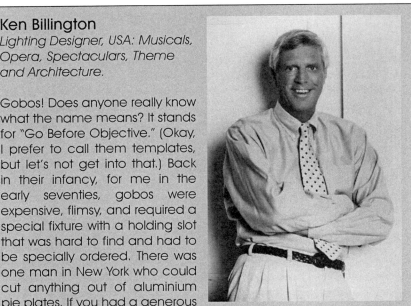

Gobos! Does anyone really know what the name means? It stands for "Go Before Objective." (Okay, I prefer to call them templates, but let's not get into that.) Back in their infancy, for me in the early seventies, gobos were expensive, flimsy, and required a special fixture with a holding slot that was hard to find and had to be specially ordered. There was one man in New York who could cut anything out of aluminium pie plates. If you had a generous budget, you could have them made of brass, but the pie plates actually held up better. Of course, if you were going to go through all this, you also had to *design* the gobo. All these complications made you consider your design very carefully and question if you really even needed a gobo. Now, a few decades later, with a catalogue full of stainless steel and glass designs, you can put a gobo in every light, but you should still question the need.

The gobos I like best are ones that do not have a round design in them. For example, Rosco 77774 Blossoms produces a great leaf design, but since the image is not round, you can project it on a surface, and it will not just look like a spotlight with a design in it. Add multiple fixtures with the same design, all rotated differently in the gobo holder, and it really creates the appearance of natural light coming through a tree.

I use gobos all the time, but an important step remains: considering if the script, scenery, and lighting support the projection of a gobo image.

7 LOOKING FORWARD…

LED Gobo Projectors

Environmental concerns have given rise to the furious development of the LED as an alternative low-energy light source. Used across both architectural and entertainment lighting, the LED populates vast swathes of tradeshow space and seems to be here to stay.

Amongst the wide choice of LED washlights, a new beast has started to appear – the LED profile or gobo projector. This can only be good news for gobos which will reap the benefits of the cool light source by prolonging gobo life in long term architectural and display installations.

David Robertson of DHA Designs says: "As architectural lighting becomes more subject to legislation and building control regulations, designers are having to find more innovative solutions with new lamp types. As fluorescent lamps are difficult to use to create dramatic lighting, LEDs are rapidly becoming the favoured source for where halogen schemes need to be replaced.

"We're already seeing the first LED gobo projectors – prohibitively expensive though they may be – which are likely to supersede bulky metal halide lanterns in architectural applications. The small size of the LED source, allied with its powerful optics and colour-changing ability, suggest a happy partnership with gobo and projection applications for years to come."

This has now begun to spill into entertainment lighting where many manufacturers have been moving towards lower energy, cooler fixtures with profile ranges such as the Philips Selecon Pacific and the LDR Soffio. One recent development, accompanied by much excitement, is that of the Robert Juliat Aledin LED profile, the first 85W LED profile with significant output and gobo projection abilities that make it a viable, energy-saving light source for entertainment environments.

It is cool enough to project 'plastic' gobos – a feature that LDR Soffio and some Selecon products are also able to do. This introduces the new possibility of designers producing their own gobos on a home printer.

Slide Film

Ironically this new development could bring about the resurgence of a technology that has suffered badly with the rise of video and digital imagery: slide film.

The quality of image attainable with home made plastic gobos is often pixelated and always far inferior to that achievable with slide film.

Similarly, the advent of powerful video projections has largely superseded slide projection because of the ease of image origination and alteration with computer graphics programmes. But neither are able to give the true black or the high resolution images possible with slide film.

LED profiles and cool running fixtures have made the reintroduce of slide materials such as Kodak Ektachrome and Duraclear and Ilford Cibachrome a feasible option with strong advantages. Cibachrome in particular is a unique material capable of prolonged use without colour degeneration, which gives a true black and can last indefinitely in an LED fixture.

As a consequence, lamp manufacturers, spurred by the growth of LEDs, are, in turn, concentrating on increasing the efficiency of tungsten halogen sources and the compact metal halide discharge lamps.

Similarly, as projector optics improve and demand better resolution from gobos, gobo manufacturers respond by continuing to improve their gobo products to keep ahead of the game and ensure a pattern of continuing improvement in quality.

Improved lantern optics have dictated a corresponding advance in gobo resolution.

Test card for monitoring more subtlety and variety on glass is now more possible than ever.

Research on glass suggests there are more improvements to come, with deeper blacks and more subtle rendering of pastels in the pipeline.

Video and Digital Gobos

So how do gobos fare against video and digital gobo technology?

Video and lighting designer Ben M Rogers believes: "The use of video is not without its drawbacks – firstly in terms of the balance and tone of the output: "video black" is not true black and, whilst there have been substantial improvements in the technology in recent years, the balance between a true black and a significant brightness is still something only truly achievable with a conventional gobo effect.

"The second drawback is the frequent complexity of user interfaces and software used in the application of digital video media for performance. The ultimate success of video as an integrated tool has as much to do with the user interface and ease of application as it does with the quality and capacity of the product."

Much of the digital gobo product revolves around a video projection system in a moving head type casing with integrated media server system or with static projectors and an external server and usually with lighting network control – highly flexible but essentially still a video source.

"The current exception is SGM's Giotto Digital Moving head profile which uses a patented DLP chip to replace the more conventional gobo module. This hybrid application of technology means that the instrument has the brightness, colour mixing, speed, zoom and dimming of a moving head but with the opportunity for the designer to load the unit with both animated and static gobos (in greyscale) to suit their needs."

So video is making in roads but its current limitations – low resolution, lack of true black, complex control systems – seems to indicate that video and more traditional gobo technology are set to continue side by side for a while yet.

Lastly, but perhaps most significantly, is the cost of video projectors and systems which, at present, put them out of reach of a large number of designers at all levels.

Gobos still present an affordable, versatile and endlessly creative designer's tool with gobo manufacturers of both metal and glass reporting continuing growth of gobo production, in spite of the recession at the time of writing.

Production times of glass gobos continue to reduce, and with the ease of artwork transmission and easy courier delivery around the world, custom gobos can be despatched quickly and globally.

We see from the Lighting Designer contributions throughout the book that designers regard gobos as an essential part of using and qualifying light, including one with 2000 custom gobos in her garage!

Donald Holder
Lighting Designer, USA: Theatre, Opera, Dance.

Gobos or templates are useful in many ways: an evocative slash of a Venetian blind across a wall, a piercing shaft of light through an overhead grating, or the image of light filtering through leaves on an actor's body can speak volumes about the context of a scene (time of day, location, emotional temperature, to name just a few possibilities).

Gobos can support the idea of light emanating from a specific source, they can soften the impact of light striking a surface when we don't want its edge to be perceived by the audience, and they can give a particularly flat wash of light more movement and depth.

Gobos can underscore the point of view or 'style' of the production: a stage picture embellished with softly dappled light will be perceived very differently than one adorned with crisp shards or slashes, for example. Like any other tool at our disposal, it's important that we're clear about why and how gobos will be used, and to understand what their particular use will imply both on an overt and subliminal level.

GOBO BASICS

Hugh Vanstone

Lighting Designer, UK: Plays, Musicals, Opera, Concerts, Industrial theatre, Architecture.

I rarely use gobos for their most obvious purpose – to project patterns. Mostly I use gobos to add texture to light. Although not always naturalistic, adding this texture can make a stage picture more interesting or dramatic, in just the same way as I would use heightened colour, for example.

I often need to use defined areas (or pools) of light on stage and gobos can be a very useful tool in "feathering out" the edges of these pools into darkness.

ML Geiger

Lighting Designer, USA: Dance, Opera, Theatre

In dance, part of what one is trying to do is reveal volume around the dancer, and to allow the space to transform. Gobos can help us shape that story – sometimes as simply as cross-fading from a tight square to a very open dappled stage and then returning again to a more confined space. Also, bodies look terrific moving through dappled light. I like the template to be something other than a circle, so use R7780 for leaves, no matter the density of the situation, because the circle of the light is not visible, and it is easier to make many units act as one.

Gobos are also an incredibly useful technical tool to make a wash feel shadowy without an obvious template. I use a large break up, or a cloud break up (R77165 or R77166) to get an asymmetrical light that can blend easily. I usually soften the light and then add R132. The point is not to perceive the template, but to have a wash that is not flat. This especially useful in front light, or a scene in which the lights are supposed to be off and there is no discernible source – and probably most useful in plays or opera.

8 GOBO USAGE

What is a Gobo?

A gobo is a lighting 'template' made from metal, glass or, with some of today's very cool-running lanterns, plastic, in which a pattern has been cut or imaged. This is placed into a profile (focusable) lantern between the light source and the lens which is then used to focus the image and project the pattern on to a surface.

Gobos for every application.

Traditionally gobos are used in theatres and clubs, in the latter often forming 'mid-air' effects as they cut through the smoke and haze. Gobos can be used to create mood, evoke a sense of location or set a scene by suggesting imagery such as foliage, flames, water, windows. Images can be specific, such as a building, tree or skyline, or simply used to texture light with abstract patterns, adding interest to surfaces, or to create effects such as dappled light through trees.

Alternatively gobos can be used as a promotional tool to promote products or companies, project messages, company logos, even directional signage such as 'Open' and 'Closed' signs, hotel room numbers and cinema screen numbers.

A wide variety of effects can be achieved with relatively few images since each gobo can be used in hard or soft focus, coloured with gel or put into various gadgets to add movement. They are an invaluable lighting aid for both the amateur and the professional, in traditional and emerging market areas. Projection effects range from the crude and obvious to tremendously subtle and sophisticated, so where do you start?

Let's start with a few basics:

How to Load a Gobo

To project a gobo successfully, a profile lantern must be used as the fixture must have the capability to focus the image being projected. I cannot be the only one (I hope!) as a student to have painstakingly cut out an intricate honeycomb design from a piece of cardboard only to wonder why it had no effect when I placed it in front of a Fresnel – other than smouldering gently in the heat. A long way to learn a short lesson!

Gobo Holders

In a standard profile lantern, the gobo must first be placed into a gobo holder – a metal affair of variable design according to manufacturer, lantern model and type of gobo used.

Some lanterns have 'sandwich' holders which capture the gobo between two joined pieces of metal; some are a single piece of metal with lugs that hold the gobo in place – the position of the lugs depending on whether a glass or metal gobo is used.

Numerous guides to gobo holder sizes, detailing which are suitable for each make and model of lantern and the size of gobo they hold, can be found on the internet. Particularly useful are those found at the White Light, Goboland, Rosco and Apollo Design Technology websites.

Glass and metal gobo holders showing lugs in different positions.

Other lanterns have integral magnetic rings which clasp the gobo into position or operate by holding the gobo in place with a spring ring pushed into an internal gobo slot.

The Right Way Up!

Whichever holder is used, one thing does not change. The gobo image is inverted by the lenses when projected, so take care to insert the gobo 'upside down and back to front' for it to read the right way up! An easy way to remember this is, if you were to look at the gobo from the position of the lamp, any writing would be upside down but facing towards you and readable from your viewing perspective.

(The only complication you might come across is if the image is being projected onto a mirror – as found in some scanners. Or if a deflector mirror is being used on the front of the lantern. Or if you are back projecting…!)

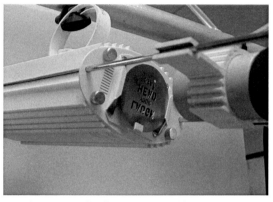

Laugh Your Head Off. Gobos should be inserted upside down and back to front

Once loaded with the gobo, the gobo holder is placed in the gobo slot of the profile lantern which is located between the light source and the lens. From this position you can focus the image to the degree of hard or soft focus that you require. Much gobo work is done using soft focus as this gives many subtle, varying results, even with relatively few gobo

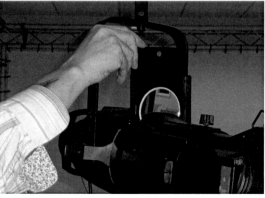

Place loaded gobo holder into gate of profile.

designs. Only specific images and text tend to be used in hard focus.

If you are using a lantern with zoom optics, you can also alter the size of the image by moving the rear lens backwards and forwards. Zoom optics are very user-friendly for this reason, and are especially useful when touring to venues with different throw distances.

Aligning Your Image

Once you have your gobo in the lantern and focused as you wish, you might want to alter the alignment of the image, say for example, to straighten a line of text. Some profiles will accommodate rotatable gobo holders which are rounded and can be rocked from side to side; alternatively many have rotating barrels which can be turned to manoeuvre the image to the required position and, if you are lucky, locked into place to prevent any further unwanted movement.

For those profiles that do not have this feature, the same realignment can be made with the addition of a Tadpole.

This is a thin ring of metal with a long handle, into which the gobo is inserted and held firm by metal clips. The gobo, which protrudes around the circumference of the Tadpole, is then inserted into a standard gobo holder and the whole unit loaded into the profile in the normal fashion. The 'tail' of the Tadpole sticks out at the top and is moved from side to side to

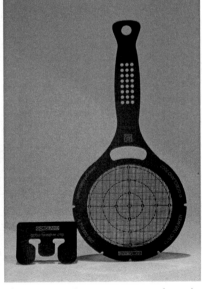

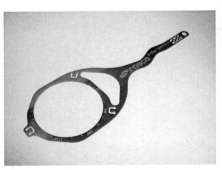

Gobos can be precisely aligned with a Tadpole.

A Gobo Tweaker incorporates the gobo design into the handle itself to form one whole unit.

rotate the gobo within the lantern until the correct alignment is achieved; the gobo is then locked in place by means of the clip on the Tadpole's tail.

If you do not have the luxury of any of these methods, some gobo manufacturers have placed a series of notches around the top half of the gobo's circumference (another good way of telling which way up your gobo should be!). These can be used to tweak the gobo's position by sticking a screwdriver down into the gobo slot – a little crude and fiddly while balancing at the top of a ladder but effective nonetheless.

Projecting a Sharp Image

So, you have your gobo loaded, focused and aligned, but perhaps the image is not as sharp as it could be? Images can suffer from an undesirable 'halo' effect which is particularly noticeable when projecting text. This is caused by interference from internal reflections within the profile and, despite the vast improvement in modern day lantern optics, this can still be a problem. There are a number of solutions to this:

Black coated gobos, as mentioned in Chapter 3, are one ready-made solution.

Butcher's Stops

Alternatively, significant improvements can be made by the simple addition of a Butcher's Stop or Donut.

This is a square of metal with a central hole that fits into the colour runner at the front of a profile. It works by removing excess light around the outer edge of the beam and optimising the more efficient light at the centre. In so doing, it lengthens the depth of field to give a clearer image across the full width of the gobo, and cuts down on unwanted reflection.

A butcher's stop or donut can be used to reduce unwanted flare around an image.

Onto its surface is etched a series of tearaway rings so that the centre of the Butcher's Stop can be removed in increments until the optimum aperture is reached. There is some dispute as to its safety since this feature tends to leave it with razor sharp edges, but the Butcher's Stop has long been an industry staple and improvised units will no doubt continue to be made by disgruntled technicians and LDs regardless! (Black wrap is a good, but rather easily trashed, alternative; cardboard is rather inflammatory!)

So now you have your gobo loaded, focused and ready to perform – so what are you going to do with it?

Gobo Uses

Gobos are now used in far more applications than the theatre and film worlds for which they were initially designed. The versatility of gobos can be seen by the sheer breadth and variety of their working environments.

- Theatre
- Opera
- Dance
- Musicals
- Museums
- Shopping malls
- Interior decorating
- Jewellery stores
- Shop windows & interiors
- Parties
- Theme parks
- Aquariums
- Art galleries
- Restaurants
- Pubs & Bars
- Hotels
- Offices
- Foyers

Martin Guerre – Prince Edward Theatre, London. sixty or more gobos (DHA 115 Dense Branches) in ETC Source 4 profiles. Lighting Designer: David Hersey.

Stage
Traditional uses within the environments of theatre, dance, opera and musicals help to set the scene, evoke an atmosphere, represent a location, such as wooded scenes, bars, city skylines and specific locations.

Architecture
Gobos are now frequently used in architectural lighting for advertising, logos, directional signage as well as adding texture and interest. This market has grown rapidly over the past 10 years with many new gobo designs and specifically designed luminaires being developed to meet demands.

Theatrical lighting techniques are being employed much more by architectural lighting designers. The use of keylights and back light to sculpt and highlight points of interest and architecture reflect the way architectural and public lighting is now an art form in itself. Buildings are treated like sculptures and shopping malls like theme parks creating an atmosphere to make shopping an 'event' or 'entertainment'.

NCR Offices, London. Lighting Design: DHA Designs. Here DHA Designs has used a dusted crystal film on the window onto which is back projected a clock effect. This serves a dual purpose of drawing attention with light yet prevents the light spilling onto the walkway.

Corporate

The corporate world holds enormous potential for custom gobos with company logos playing a large part in the branding at conferences, product launches and the like, many of which reach the level of full scale productions in themselves. This is precision work where accuracy and clarity of image is of paramount importance.

Exhibition

Gobos are a popular means of providing a theatrical approach to exhibition work. This use of foliage gobos at the Imperial War Museum helped to create the impression of moonlight shining through the trees.

Royal Navy, HMI Illustrious, Remembrance Day Ceremony 2006, Greenwich.

Adam Grater
Lighting Designer, UK: Theatre, Exhibitions, Architectural and Corporate.

My first serious gobo encounter was in the mid seventies – John Spradbery's lighting of *A Midsummer Night's Dream* for Lindsay Kemp: a richly coloured, densely textured organic swirl of a lighting design, which obscured almost as much as it revealed and gave the audience wonderful shadowy glimpses into a mysterious world.

So, I took a few out with me on some rock and roll tours, wedged into old Lekos between the rows of Parcans on pre-rigged trussing. I found a few non-specific shafts of light could really transform a ballad, making the somewhat precarious exercise of on-truss profile focusing worth the effort.

"Some years on, working in the design studio at DHA, I got to know a lot more about gobos, in both hard and soft focus, and at all points in between. If it wasn't in the catalogue we would make it: for example, the original Reflected Water (now Rosco 77903) was artworked by Vicky Fairall from a holiday snap of the play of light over the hull of a Greek fishing boat. We first used it on an industrial for Vickers submarines.

"When we set up the architectural lighting studio in the 80s we had a lot of clients wanting "theatrical lighting" (whatever that is!) for exhibition and display projects, and subsequently many a dull surface has been transformed by a softly textured play of light.

My favourite gobo? It has to be the DHA glass moon (now Rosco 82700). It can make the hairs on the back of my neck stand up.

Further enhancement could be achieved by placing Animation Units (see Chapter 11) on the front of the lanterns to create the impression of the branches moving in the breeze.

Imperial War Museum, London. Exhibition: The 1940's House. Lighting design: Alison Proctor. Photograph White Light.

Photography

One field in sharp decline for gobo use is that of photography. Gobo projected backdrops were once employed as a faster and more economical means of providing backgrounds for photographic shoots than the more traditional patterns cloths, but with the advent of digital photography, these have largely been superseded by digital manipulation.

So far we have referred only to static gobo images. In Chapter 11 we will be dealing with some of the devices that can be used to give movement – or at least the impression of movement – to these static images.

Andy Grant
Lighting Designer, UK:
Corporate Events.

Corporate gobos generally need to be used in a much more precise fashion than, for example, in theatre. I normally project them on to walls where it is important they are aligned correctly and any keystoning corrected for at the artwork stage.

Much of what I do is new product or brand launches where the client has spent a large amount of money

on expensive re-branding so it is imperative I don't distort the gobo image outside the brand guidelines. Some companies are more relaxed than others and will allow their logo to be rotated or projected at jaunty angles.

However, if the "brand police" do not agree to this, they sometimes allow me to take a section of the logo – such as the beak of a bird or an element of a design – and create a gobo from that.

For example, one client, a Qatari aluminium company, has for its logo a watermark of the atomic structure of aluminium. I took this part of the branding, made a repeat pattern out of it, and used this as a break-up gobo on some stage tabs. A nice bit of subtle branding, I thought!

Peter Mumford

Lighting Designer, UK: Dance, Opera, Drama, Television.

Well, although I do use gobos from time to time, from a design point of view I think one has to be careful. The areas where, for me, they are at their most useful and usable is where the resulting light is an accurate representation of what light does when it passes through a structure, a window or a tree for example. The more abstract shapes and patterns and swirls I generally leave to events such as the Eurovision Song Contest, etc!

There are now some new and interesting textures though. I used 'Abstract Weave' and 'Ink Roller' – both DHA (now Rosco 76595 and 76602 respectively) quite extensively in a production of *Midsummer Marriage* in Chicago creating a textured cyc behind Alison Chitty's set of hundreds of vertical rods.

*Production Photo: **Midsummer Marriage**, Chicago Lyric Opera, 2005. Designer: Alison Chitty. Director: Sir Peter Hall. Lighting design and photo: Peter Mumford.*

9 GOBO TYPES

Gobo Sizes

Gobos have been produced in many sizes over the years of development with a tendency for more standardisation now than before. Sizing is critical and much research has gone into achieving the maximum light clearance within the minimum space and to allow for the greatest possible detail in image design. It is a finely balanced equation.

The most popular standard sizes are:

Gobo Size (mm)	Gobo Diameter (mm)	Image Diameter
A	100	68-75
B	86	64.5
M	65.5	49.5
D	53.3	40
E	37.5	24 – 28.13

Moving lights often take smaller or non-standard sizes. Past sizes have ranged from the enormous 150mm C size down to the diminutive 25mm Vari*Lite VL1 size, with some moving lights even smaller.

Some manufacturers prefer gobos to be ordered by this alphabetical size reference. Most catalogue designs are identified by this size reference, followed by a code number and name. Goboland have their own system of categorisation where by not only size and design are delineated by number, but also material and gobo 'family' or category.

The DHA range of designs is easily translated into Rosco design numbers by the addition of '77' in front of the old DHA numbers. There are some exceptions, but this is a good rule of thumb that will make both ranges of designs easily accessible, whichever catalogue you are working from.

Gobo Materials

Gobo materials fall roughly into the following categories: metal, glass, dichroic, plastic, digital. Choosing which material best suits your purpose relies not only on desired result and available budget but, a crucial factor, the temperature of the fixture.

Some lanterns, whilst having a great light output, are 'gobo eaters' as the intense heat burns and bends the gobo in a relatively short time. Fixtures pre-dating the ETC Source 4, the first of the cooler running lanterns, would run at such high temperatures that the gobo would come out of the gate literally glowing red hot – an interesting challenge when doing fast gobo changes during training workshops and the reason why many gobo salesmen and technicians have no fingerprints and asbestos fingers!

Today's lanterns, such as the ETC Source 4 and the Philips Selecon Pacific, are becoming cooler and more efficient, generating less heat in the gobo gate. Now, LED innovations, such as Robert Juliat's Aledin, give more output for less power consumption, improving the green credentials of our often power-hungry industry, and combining high quality projection optics and high light output with low energy costs and a lower environmental impact.

Metal Gobos

Large catalogues of designs have been built up based on metal gobo designs. Companies such as Rosco, DHA Lighting, Apollo Design Technology, GAM and Lee Filters, to name but a few, are a rich source of readily available gobo designs to professional and amateur alike.

Metal gobos have been dealt with in detail in Chapter 3, but here we recap on their advantages and disadvantages:

Advantages:
- Available in a variety of materials including stainless steel, nickel silver, black coated steel, aluminium, phosphor bronze, nickel silver, brass, to suit application
- Economical enough for mass use and repeat use.
- Large number of catalogue designs readily available
- Do not break when dropped!

Disadvantages:
- Designs must be 'tagged' to prevent island areas from dropping out
- No colour unless added by filter
- Resolution is limited, especially in smaller sizes

Glass Gobos

A significant amount has already been written in Chapter 5 about the manufacture of glass gobos, both monochrome, dichroic spot colour and full CYMK colour mixing.

Advantages

- Higher resolution images possible than with metal, even photographic quality
- Monochrome, tonal images, spot and full colour all possible
- No tags or bridges in the design

Disadvantages

- Breakable and do not like being dropped
- Limited heat tolerance, although this has improved tremendously in conjunction with improved heat management in lanterns

There are a number of things you can do to reduce these risks.

Looking After Your Glass Gobo

Glass Gobos need special care due to their fragile nature!

1. Flat field the lantern

Before putting the gobo into the luminaire, adjust the lamp in the reflector to produce an even beam of light. If this is not done and hotspots are allowed to occur, the glass will not be heated evenly across its surface, placing uneven stress on the substrate which may cause it to break.

2. Clean the Gobo

Polish the glass with a soft cloth to remove greasy fingerprints and always handle glass gobos by their edge. Greasy fingerprints can again cause an uneven build up of heat across the gobo surface and run the risk of the gobo cracking.

Look after your glass gobos and you will get along swimmingly!
'Fish Art' Saturated colour and pastels. Courtesy of Prosperity, Hong Kong.

3. Place the coated surface away from the lamp
(Some manufacturers advise otherwise – always check with your manufacturer before use.)

This reduces the risk of the coating being damaged by heat and peeling off. It also means the heat can pass through the gobo and does not get bounced back into lamp and increase the internal temperature.

4. Allow room for glass expansion
When using a glass gobo holder, check the lugs to ensure there is a 1mm gap between the gobo and each lug to allow for expansion as the glass warms up. If the lugs are too tight and are allowed to press against the heated gobo, the glass will crack.

5. Pre-warm the glass
Where possible, 'toast' the gobo by warming it on a low level (10% or 20%) before gently bringing the light level up to full. By not subjecting the glass to sudden changes in temperature you are reducing the risk of breakage.

Bezels

Special care should be taken when using a glass gobo in a metal bezel. Bezels are used for a number of reasons: the gobo may be a full colour gobo made of several layers of glass which are too thick to fit under the lugs of a standard glass gobo holder; a smaller size of glass, for example an M size (for gobo sizes see page 99), may be used to optimise the central part of the beam yet is required for use in a profile which only

Glass gobos are often mounted in bezels.

takes a B size; a bezel may be used to cut down on the reflection caused by several layers of glass.

Whatever the reason, when ordering your gobo be careful to specify:
- which lantern you are using
- whether there is a mirror inside (eg scanner) or outside (eg Rosco

I-Cue, the automated deflector mirror) the lantern so the manufacturer can make your gobo with the coated surface in the correct orientation.

Hints and Tips

Some gobos have very reflective surfaces, some have matt surfaces – it is not always obvious which is the coated side. An easy way to check which side is the coated side is to place the tip of a pen on the glass gobo. If there is a gap between the pen tip and the reflection, the coating is on the opposite side.

Alternative Glass Gobos

There are more types of glass 'gobo' which do not fall into the 'imaged' category. These are variously textured and coloured glass which lend another creative dimension to the designer's palette. They have a number of different trade names, depending on manufacturer, which can be a little confusing but are worth exploring.

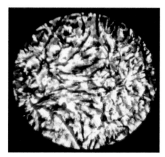

Colorizers (Rosco) – Painted, stippled effects on a flat glass base add multi-coloured interest when used in conjunction with metal patterns. Effects are more intricate than those achievable with single gel filters (top).

Prismatics (Rosco), Crushed Dichroics (Apollo Design Technology) – are multi-coloured gobos made from chips of coloured dichroic glass, stuck to a glass base (clear or sometimes coloured) to form a textured pattern. Try combining two in a double gobo rotator or use in soft focus behind a metal stained glass window gobo (centre).

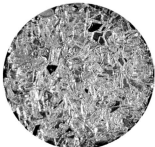

Image Glass (Rosco), Textured Glass (Apollo Design Technology) – deeply textured glass that refracts and bends light and can be used as a pattern in its own right or in combination to animate standard gobo images (right).

ColorWaves (Rosco), Textured Dichroic (Apollo Design Technology) – a textured patterned glass base is coated with a coloured dichroic layer to combine the effects of both texture and colour creating a gobo that is especially effective when used in kinetic effects such as gobo rotators.

Plastic Gobos

Plastic gobos can be used in a limited number of fixtures and are generally only suitable for short-term applications.

Advantages
- Cheap
- Quickly made on basic office printer
- No chemicals used in manufacture

Disadvantages
- Pixelated/poor quality image
- No true black
- Plastic, so how environmentally friendly are they?

Fixtures:
- Philips Selecon
- LDR Soffio
- Robert Juliat Aledin LED Profile
- ETC Source 4, if used in conjunction with a Rosco iPro unit.

Products

Rosco ImagePro (iPro) – Fan cooled carrier of plastic slides/gobos. Fits the effects slot of ETC Source 4, Altman Shakespeare, Philips Selecon Pacific or Strand SL. Heat management handled by a combination of a cooling airflow across the surface of the slide, infrared reflection and thermal barriers. Slide lasts for 15-20 hours depending on colours (dark blue will burn out faster than yellow, for example).

Fergo Plastic Projections – Designed by David Ferguson in New Zealand, Fergo Plastic Projections have been at the forefront of developing plastic projections since September 1998.

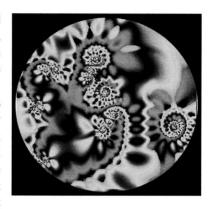

Primarily designed for use in Philips Selecon Pacific, a Fergo is basically a high temperature, high resolution transparency with a dense black and rich saturated colours. Fergos combine well with Rosco iPro and are aimed at giving low cost image access on short seasons or as required by quick turnaround and budget limitations.

Luci della Ribalta (LDR) Gobo Wizard – Software for creating and printing customised plastic gobos.

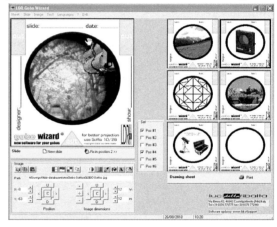

Based on an idea by Fabiano Besio, the Gobo Wizard is a unique software for making custom plastic gobos. Designed specially for the LDR Soffio profile and products using M and D size gobos, it takes imported images and turns them into colour photographs. These can be printed on standard OHP acetate film using a standard ink-jet or laser printer.

Images and text are self aligned in the centre of the gobo but can be re-sized, mirrored and turned at will.

Digital Gobos

Digital gobos are something that have been talked about, researched and showcased for a number of years. The Medusa Icon M claimed to be the first 'digital light' and contained the entire DHA Lighting gobo catalogue in digital format. High End Catalyst followed close behind, with both spearheading the beginnings for integration of a new way of lighting.

From here a whole new industry of video design has emerged which is developing fast, although occasionally difficult to classify with 'video design' often falling to the lighting designer by default. But a new breed of video designer is coming into being and a range of products, such as the media servers from the likes of Green Hippo, Arkaos, Martin Professional and Projected Image, to name but a few, is developing in parallel.

"Manufacturers frequently strive to build as much capacity into the products to give users an ever expanding palette of options in the same way that technology is continually pushed by users at the cutting edge of design." says video designer, Ben M Rogers.

"From a design perspective therefore we need to approach the implementation of video as a digital lighting instrument with precision, choosing carefully those elements which are most appropriate to create the effect and mood and not be romanced by the potential of the technology, but be disciplined to know what best serves the needs of the performance – as the saying goes, "just because we can doesn't mean we should".

Peggy Eisenhauer
Lighting Designer, USA:
Theatre, Musical, Film.

From my perspective, using a gobo image in lighting design offers a way of filtering the audiences' visibility. I imagine an indefinite space between  the eyes of the audience and the space on stage as a theatrical lens which they see through. I often use gobo projection as a lens through which the audience sees the play, as though they are seeing through something with shape, depth, structure, and texture.

10 CUSTOM GOBOS AND HOW TO ORDER THEM

One of the enduring images of the Vancouver Winter Olympics was the Sails of Light show, titled "Look At The Games". With 200 million people watching on TV, those colours on the gobo projections better be right!

There are now thousands of readily available gobo designs, in metal and glass, to chose from the catalogues of several gobo manufacturers. But having your own customised gobo design made to order is a very popular choice.

Before the internet, artwork was either sent as 'camera-ready' or faxed with as high resolution as possible. Customers have even been known to send items such as beer and champagne bottles with the instructions to make a gobo of the logo!

Typically, in the early days of custom gobos, delivery time of metal gobos, was 3-5 days but this has progressively reduced and faster turnaround times are now the norm.

To ensure you receive the precise gobo design you ordered and in the shortest time possible, it is important to give the manufacturer as much accurate information as possible. Precise details vary from manufacturer to manufacturer, who are generally very willing to guide you through the process, but this is a basic guide of what to consider when commissioning your own design.

Lantern
Specify lantern make, model and focal length so the manufacturer can be sure they make the gobo to the correct size for the fixture. NB some lanterns require non-standard image sizes.

Material
Specify metal, monochrome glass, spot colour glass or full colour CYMK glass according to your requirements. Your manufacturer will be able to advise you if you are unsure.

Gobo Size and Image Size
Always include the gobo diameter (A size, B size etc) and image size required in millimeters (mm). Be realistic about how much detail can fit onto the gobo surface – the smaller the gobo the lower the effective resolution.

Light/Dark
Specify which areas of the design are required for projection. Areas etched away will equal light.

Keystoning
If distortion correction of the image is required to compensate for an offset projector position, supply the manufacturer with measurements for the vertical and horiontal position of the fixture in relation to the projection surface, and the throw distance. More detail on keystone correction can be found in Chapter 4.

Mirror or Front/Back Projection
The orientation of the gobo projection is affected by the addition of a mirror (either within the fixture such as a scanner or added to the

front as a deflector, such as a Derksen Gobo Top or Rosco I-Cue). Similarly it is important to specify if the gobo is to be front or back projected so the manufacturer can incorporate this into their calculations.

Rotation
If the gobo image is to be used in a rotator, mark the required centre of rotation on the image.

Composite
State whether the design is to be part of a composite image.

Quantity, Delivery Date and Address
Finally, of course, state clearly the quantity, required delivery date and delivery address. Gobos are often ordered with a short deadline and delivered

Predistortion of the artwork allowed this gobo to be projected onto the hotel frontage from a luminaire at ground level. Photo: Ivo Dielen, Goboland.

direct to site so make sure these last minute details are as accurate as possible.

Repeat Orders
It is worth remembering that most companies store custom gobo designs for many years so that customers can place repeat orders quickly and economically.

Artwork Guidelines
The better the quality of artwork, the better the gobo result.
For electronic artwork transmission here are some guidelines.
- Adobe Illustrator or Adobe Acrobat are preferred for logos and all fonts should be converted to outline before submission.

- Adobe Photoshop or a similar photo processing application is preferred for photographic style images.
- Formats: pdf, TIFF, eps, ai, psd, bmp, dmx gif and png are all possible, although jpg should be avoided.
- Background: gobo projection works best when projecting images out of a black background.
- For high quality, full colour gobos, a good rule of thumb is to submit 1800 x 1800 pix files. Almost any file format is acceptable, but WordArt and CAD files should be avoided.

Mark Stanley
Lighting Designer, USA: Dance, Opera, Theatre, Television

The choice of using a gobo is about two things: What does the beam of light look like in the air, and what does it look like on the surface that the light illuminates?

I am always looking for ways to control, manipulate and enhance texture in light in these two places. For me, a beam of light remains just that, until you add a template. It transforms the light into something more organic, three dimensional  and alive, and it enables the light to become an integral and specific part of the composition. Surfaces come to life with the layers and enhanced contrasts that light from a template provides.

I rarely use templates to project a realistic image. Occasionally there might be the call for a graphic pattern or a leaf image on a window, scrim, or drop, but for me, the real enjoyment of designing with a template is in the modelling and subtle (or overt) contrasts that it brings to the stage.

Photo by Rosalie O'Connor.

11 GOBO GISMOS

Moving Effects Projection and its Provenance

We have shown in Chapter 1 the early development of the Magic Lantern; some effects were designed to produce movement and many of these are the inspiration and origins of present day techniques.

We pick a few to illustrate.

Pepper's Ghost

This was an invention of John Pepper shown at the Royal Polytechnic in London. A ghost illusion was produced by reflecting the static or moving image of an actor concealed from audience view in an area below the stage. The actor was brightly lit, at that time by a limelight lantern, and a large angled sheet of glass was placed at the front of the stage; so the

Pepper's Ghost.

ELECTRIC STAGE EFFECTS

Cut to left shows our effect with Lense No. 626 and No. 629 attached.

All of our effects are original and are equipped with every mechanical and optical contrivance known that will project an effect as realistic as possible. Our effects are generally made on a single mica disc, 18 inches in diameter, enclosed in a sheet iron case, and operated by a clock movement from the center. Where certain effects require 2 discs in one case, or where others require two machines, we specify same below, after the title name of such effects. Each effect, when equipped with one of our Sciopticon Condenser Holder No. 629 can be slipped on or off our standard 5 or 6-inch spot lamps very quickly.

Cut above shows an effect with Lenses No. 627 and No. 629 mounted on a spot lamp.

As there are many who may use two or more effects, but not all at the same time, they can no doubt get along with only one set of lenses, by using this one set on all the effects. For this reason we quote prices below on our effects complete without Sciopticon Condenser Holder No. 629 and Sciopticon Objective No. 626. The effects as quoted below include the effect painted on a mica disc, which is enclosed in a metal case, and a clock movement, which is also enclosed in a metal case.

Cat. No.		Price	Code Word
564	Avalanche Effect	$ 85.00	bulk
565	Aeroplanes Flying	100.00	bull
566	American Flag Waving	40.00	buoy
567	Aurora Borealis Rays (8 in. double disc) .	75.00	burn
568	Blizzard Effect	85.00	bury
569	Burning Forest	95.00	bush
570	Climbing Monkey	110.00	bust
571	Crawling Spiders (for 2 machines)	90.00	busy
572	Cyclone	80.00	buys
573	Cyclone with flying objects (double disc)	120.00	buzz
574	Electric Fountain Effect	95.00	cabs
575	Falling Flowers	120.00	cads
576	Falling Leaves	120.00	cafe
577	Falling Roses	120.00	cage
578	Falling Star (hand movement)	15.00	cake
579	Fireworks Effect	85.00	calk
580	Flame Effect	80.00	calm
581	Flowing Water	80.00	cane

Electric stage effects late twenties catalogue.

audience saw a composite view of the actor on stage reflected on the inclined glass.

The idea is still in use today, and can be found in the National Sports Museum in Melbourne Australia, Blenheim Palace, the Dickens World attraction at Chatham and in Dover Castle.

Electric Stage Effects

By the late 1920s in the USA there were several 'electric stage effects' notably in the Chicago Stage Lighting Co catalogue.

A 19" mica disc is painted with the effect and 60 effects are listed with the rather high prices of up to $120, and differing effects for two or three 'machines'. These discs are mounted on a floor mounted arc sourced spot. The disc motor was clockwork driven.

In the same catalogue, the curiously named Lobsterscope is a rotating disc with two irregular shaped apertures mounted in a metal case which can be rotated at varying geared speeds by hand. It is really an early 'strobe' effect generator as it was described as a flicker effect, which when used on a dance troupe, for instance, produces the 'startling and weird' effect of increasing speed of movement of the dancers.

The Linnebach Projector
Named after Adolph Linnebach, Technical Director of the Munich

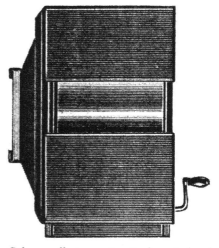

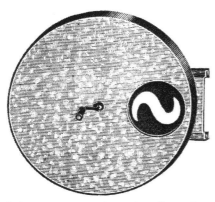

Lobsterscope – early strobe effect – late twenties.

Colour effects spot attachment hand lever operated sunrise/sunset effect from micadisc. Late twenties.

Opera House from 1923 to 1944, this is essentially shadow projection from a black painted lensless lantern. Shadow casting had long been an entertainment, there are records of 'shadow-shows' in the 1600s in London and Paris. It was sufficiently popular for Strand in England to name a projector Pattern N623 as a Linnebach and some of the US lantern makers marketed Linnebach projectors.

Cloud and Water Movement

Several companies, like Schwabe and Reiche and Vogel had versions of cloud projections.

By the 1930s Strand in England were producing moving effects of flames, waves and clouds with images on mica – the best heat resistant medium available until the post war development of heat resistant glass – with rotation provided by a clockwork motor.

By 1966 Francis Reid was introducing gobo movement effects for *Turn of the Screw* at Morley College using a pair of Pattern 23/Ns with motorised colour wheels. Fortunately the fixed speed of the rotating colour wheels tallied with the rhythm of Britten's horse drawn coach.

A new form of gobo projection?

The 1972 Strand catalogue shows 12 moving effect types on 18¾" discs for their Pattern 252 2kW 'optical effects' projector.

All of these have bearing on present day motion effects and in this chapter we will show how simple rotation and animation effects can be achieved.

Creating Movement

In Chapter 8 we showed how to load, project and focus a static gobo image. Now we can take it a stage further by adding movement to light using a few easily available tools. We are not referring to moving head lanterns which physically move a gobo image around a room, but to the gadgets that can be added to a profile lantern to lend that extra dimension of movement to a static image (although some of these effects have now been incorporated into moving head technology).

Light attracts the eye but motion also attracts attention – a combination of the two is very arresting. A poster may attract the attention but a moving poster catches the eye compelling you to look at it – it is the same with a moving projected image, adding interest and drawing the attention – whether it be in an office reception or at a trade show, a club or, more subtly, in a theatre environment with the reflection of water, movement of tree branches or even glowing embers of fire.

As a promotional tool projected images are a powerful medium and gobos are used increasingly in retail and public environments. For example, attract someone in to shop, museum or restaurant by sweeping a logo through a doorway using a revolving barrel mirror such as those manufactured by Derksen, or run it along an aisle to direct customers to where you want them to be. Project onto a wall at height to attract customers from a distance above the busy foreground areas of a shop. Alternatively project a revolving logo on the pavement using the movement to catch the peripheral vision. This way it will even attract the eye of someone walking by with their head down!

So what do we use to achieve some of these effects? Roughly speaking, moving effects can be divided into two kinds:

Gobo Rotators
Animation Units

The first group includes single and double gobo rotators, and their derivatives such as Indexers, Yoyos, X-Effects and Prismo and are based around the concept of rotating a static image situated, with the exception of the Prismo, between the lamp and the lens.

The second group includes animation units and discs and rely upon the interaction between a static gobo image and a moving disc placed on the front of the lantern. A variation of this is the GAM Film effect (see p 131).

With the prevalence of moving lights, these may appear a little archaic, but the simplicity by which a profile lantern can be transformed into something more than a static gobo projector, the ease of use, the pre-existance of equipment already to hand, and the economy of the system all render them relevant today.

Besides, their influence in moving light development is undeniable as rotation and indexing are now basic attributes within moving lights whilst animation principles have also been transposed in the form of miniature animation wheels in, for example, Martin Professional MAC 2000 Performance II units.

Benefits of Moving Effects

There are several benefits to using moving effects:

- Economy – rotators, animation units and the like fit a wide range of existing profile lanterns so many effects can be created without having to invest in more expensive effects projectors or moving heads.

- Flexibility – completely new effects can be achieved simply by changing the gobo or, in the case of the animation unit, the effects disc.

- Experimentation – you cannot get a true representation of a moving effect from a catalogue or a book! So you need to try it out for yourself. For example, subtle variations can be achieved by changing the speed of movement, the focus of the lantern or the orientation of the motion.

- Simplicity – it ain't rocket science! Despite the number of variations and choices, a short time spent trying out the gadgets should go a long way to de-mystifying the whole concept of moving effects. You will be surprised how quickly you gain a good understanding of how to create the effects you want with only a few pieces of equipment and some gobos.

Gobo Rotators
Single Gobo Rotator

A single gobo rotator does exactly what it says – it enables a single gobo to be rotated about its central axis at speeds of between 0 – 20 rpm.

Methods of loading vary according to manufacturer (eg DHA/Rosco Single Gobo Rotator, Apollo Design Technologies Simply Single) but generally the gobo can be either metal or glass, normally B size, although M size or even D size have been made. It is loaded into the gobo rotator from the back and, if metal, held in place by a retaining ring which serves the dual purpose

*The need for a revolving chess board projection to follow the movement of the massive hydraulic chess board in the stage in the 1986 West End production of **Chess The Musical** gave rise to the creation of the DHA Gobo Rotator.*

of holding gobo in place and reducing any distortion of gobo caused by heat. It is finally secured with a retaining spring which slots into a groove around the inner edge of the rotator cavity. The retaining ring is not required when using a glass gobo since the thickness of the glass is sufficient to stop the gobo from moving under the spring.

Same rules apply as for a static gobo about which way round the gobo should be loaded although of course, alignment and orientation are not important since the gobo will be rotating. The whole lot is then loaded into the lantern's wide 'effects slot'.

NB: Always load the rotator with the motor housing facing forward and away from the lamp housing. The latter is the hottest part of the lantern and can cause heat damage to the motor if loaded incorrectly.

Fixed speed units which rotated at 0.25/ 1/ 2/ 5/ 10rpm have been largely superseded by variable speed rotators and most are both DMX controllable and/or have on-board switches which can be used to change the speed or direction of movement and give stand alone control.

David Hersey
Lighting Designer, USA and UK:
Theatre, Musicals, Opera, Ballet.

Textured light has become a big part of the lighting vocabulary. Some productions require extensive use of gobos and, of course, some require no gobos at all.

I started making gobos out of the frustration of not being able to have the detailed break up patterns that I saw in nature and wanted to be able to use on the stage.

The gobo rotator was born because, when I was lighting *Chess* in 1986, I needed to have indexing squares of light which could register on a full-stage revolving chess board. Then the "Yoyo" was developed because I needed a door opening effect. Its linear movement also made simple water effects possible.

Today, many of these devices have been incorporated into the bewildering morass of moving lights now available to the designer.

It's been an interesting journey going from gobos made from aluminium pie plates with holes stabbed in them to the full-colour, perfect register, glass gobos available now. We used to have to accept many limitations when we began a lighting design; now we start with a truly blank sheet of paper."

Hints and Tips
Good gobos to use in single rotators for maximum effect are spiral patterns such as Rosco 77761 Spiral, or 77891 Laser Line which is particularly effective as a mid air effect through haze. (See the Gobo Families chapter at the end of the book for more examples from a variety of manufacturers.)

Manufacturers give fitting references to show which rotators fit which makes of lantern, with many concentrating on the cooler running, lower wattage models since they are kinder to the gobo rotator mechanism and the gobo itself.

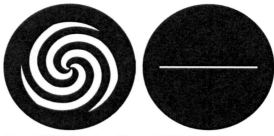

Rosco 77761 Spiral and Rosco 77891 Laser Line.

Double Gobo Rotator

A double gobo rotator allows two B size gobos – metal or glass – to be rotated about their common central axis with spectacular results. Some double gobo rotators are quite simple and only rotate in opposite directions at the same speed, controlled by a single motor and one channel of DMX, or by control switches on the motor housing. Others, notably the DHA (now Rosco) Double Gobo Rotator, run off two channels of DMX (one for each gobo) allowing *independent* control of both speed and direction of each gobo. This gives finer control and therefore considerably more creative possibilities.

Gobos are loaded from both front and back, but otherwise in the same manner as a single gobo rotator.

However, in a double rotator, the retaining rings now provide three spacing options when using metal gobos. This can be exploited for artistic effect or to prevent mechanical intervention. If both gobos are inserted first with retaining rings placed on top, the gobos will be less than 1.5mm apart enabling both to be in sharp focus. At the opposite extreme, retaining rings can be inserted first thus spacing the gobos several millimetres apart from each other. This can prevent fine design gobos from entangling with each other or even enable one gobo to 'animate' the second 'off-focus' gobo (see section on Animation).

Rosco Vortex 360. Double gobo rotators are marketed by several companies under various names including GAM Twin-Spin, Rosco Vortex 360, Apollo Smart Move, etc.

Hints and Tips

Gobo choice

Conventional rotation designs work well: gobos such as two B77392 Geometric 2 placed in opposite directions or two B77568 Spira Gira are effective here. But don't be bound by the conventional when using rotation.

Rosco 77392 Geometric 2. Rosco 77634 Vanishing Squares.

Try some different and unlikely combinations such as two B77634 Vanishing Squares, two B78124 Sparkles or even two B77546 Scrub inserted in opposition to each other for surprising effects. This shows how some incredibly complex effects can be achieved using very simple and economical technology.

Adding colour

Use split gel in strong colours to emphasise dramatic psychedelic effects. Alternatively use coloured and textured dichroic glass gobos to add colour and motion.

Fire Effect: A simple projected image can be made more interesting by simply adding colour whilst texture provides an extra dimension of movement to add yet more realism

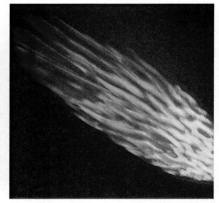

Rosco ColorWaves, Amber Ripple projected obliquely, can be combined with a Cyan Ripple for myriad colour combinations.

Try experimenting with images in soft focus to create more interesting effects by playing on the badly focused part of the optics. The subsequent refraction of light can be used to great advantage by adding textured and coloured dichroic glass to colour the image – or even just a combination of coloured, textured glass. Refraction causes the colours to be mixed within the image, especially with the more abstract designs, and can give rise to many different effects by such a simple process.

Software

There are a number of Program/Apps on the market which enable you to combine gobo images in a virtual 'rotator'. This lets you explore ideas and have an indication of the results you can achieve without having the actual equipment to hand. Check out GAM Products *Virtual TwinSpin*, and Wybron's *Moiré Gobo Library*, available as an iPhone App, for a start.

Indexer

Two products that evolved from the rotator concept, initially from the David Hersey stable, are the Indexer and the YoYo.

The Indexer (now Rosco Indexing Rotator) is an indexable version of the standard gobo rotator (single or double) with on-board DMX. It sought to achieve for standard profiles what moving light manufacturers were also working on – the ability to precisely control the position and movement of a rotating image.

It bears all the attributes of standard rotators in terms of fitting and focusing options, but offers the additional facility of programming cue sequences which can be triggered by DMX, and runs off a colour-scroller compatible power supply. Operationally quiet and durable, it is ideal for permanent and multiple installations such as theme parks, retail environments and trade shows.

Rosco Indexing Rotator.

Hints and Tips
Indexers can be programmed to behave as a Real Time Clock.

Yoyo
Originally using conventional gobos, the Yoyo was redesigned to take specially etched effects plates which move an image in and out of the gate of a lantern in a linear motion. Available as single or double units, images interact with each other to create movements such as water ripples, or act as a basic gobo changer where one image is withdrawn from the gate and replaced by a second.

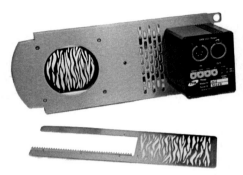

The need for the effect of light spill from an opening and closing door gave birth to the DHA Yo-yo.

Fitting only a handful of profiles (ETC Source 4, Altman Shakespeare, Strand SL and, with restriction, Philips Selecon Pacific), the Yoyo works along similar lines to the indexing rotator giving full control over the distance of travel and precise position of each plate within the gate. A 'stand alone' option is also available for simple linear motion or long term installation, such as retail or display purposes, where the effect can be pre-programmed and left to run.

Both the Yoyo and Apollo Design Technology's Smart Move Vertical can also take a conventional metal gobo in the built-in holder on the back plate.

Effects can be programmed to happen over a long period of time (between one second and 255 minutes – four hours 15 minutes) and are especially effective if used in conjunction with a split colour filter.

Uses have included the rising sun in *Miss Saigon* at London's Theatre Royal Drury Lane in 1989.

Hints and Tips
Yoyo effects plates should be stored flat to prevent bending which might cause operational problems. They are also very thin and sharp and appear to work quite successfully as a cigar cutter!

Innumerable other gobo gizmos exist and thankfully we have the internet to scour for them. For reasons of space, only a selection can be printed here.

GAM Prismo

This is a rotating prism which fits in the colour runner of an ETC Source 4 profile and multiplies the gobo image three or five times depending on the choice of prism.

GAM Prismo.

Variations can be achieved by altering focus and adding colours to the surface of the prism or to the colour runner behind it. It can also be used in conjunction with a gobo rotator since it sits at the front of the lantern.

It has been designed primarily for live shows, display, museums and theme parks.

Rosco X24 X-Effects

The X24 X-Effects projector uses two glass gobos which, rather than rotating around the same axis, are set off-centre, crossing each other only at the centre of the beam to give effects without visible direction or pattern. Arguably the Rosco X24 X-Effects unit does not fit into this chapter as it is a custom built projector rather than an accessory for a profile lantern, but it shows the development of ideas and its technology has undoubtedly come from the gobo rotator principle.

Rosco X24 X-Effects.

Nick Schlieper
Lighting Designer, Australia:
Theatre, Opera, Dance.

My first response to the subject of gobos would be: *"don't like 'em, hardly ever use 'em!"*

This statement, however, is wildly incorrect. I doubt there's a cloud gobo in the catalogue that I haven't used and I've certainly tried many of the available windows and blinds. When Rosco released the 'Image Glass' range, I fell in love with those and have used them frequently.

This contradiction is informative on the subject of gobo use. The first statement applies to the idea of projecting a rather "bald" and simplified outline image onto a stage. The truth however, is that they are an enormously useful tool when it comes to enriching the *texture* of light and with the wide range available nowadays, these possibilities are endless.

Jennifer Tipton
Lighting Designer, USA: Theatre, Dance, Ballet.

I use gobos in five basic ways when lighting the stage: for the graphic picture that a gobo can give whether it be a picture, a word or light through a window or door; for the sense of broken light coming through leaves, cracks in a fence, etc; to soften a hard lightline on a wall or another piece of scenery; to use as an aperture instead of an iris; to represent glints of light that are thrown about a room from shiny objects in that room. This is a useful way to light a space so objects and actors are visible without lighting the entire stage.

Animation Effects

Animation effects – or KK wheels, Rosco Infinity, DHA Animation Unit – seem to have developed from the zooscope principles described in earlier chapters. Basically an animation system, it creates moving images based on a static gobo in a standard profile lantern, with an animation wheel located in front of the lantern instead of inside the gate.

The effects can be changed from flames to rippling water, clouds to snow or rain, simply by changing the gobo or the animation disc.

The whole animation principle is based on three changeable components:

The Gobo
The Animation Unit
The Animation Disc

It works by the animation disc at the front of the lantern breaking up the beam created by the gobo in the lantern gate, so that only part of the image is displayed at any one time. As the wheel rotates different parts of the image are displayed in turn creating the illusion of motion.

The Animation Unit

Animation units were once available to fit most lanterns and are easier to size than a rotator since it was simply a case of measuring the colour frame of the lantern. The reference number of the AMU generally relates to the size, in mm, of the colour frame of a lantern. For example, Selecon Pacific has a colour frame of 185mm and therefore takes an AMU185. However, be warned that some manufacturers now restrict themselves to fitting only the most popular profile lanterns.

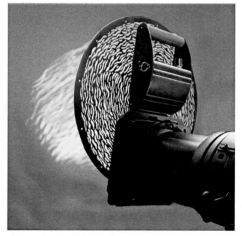

The Disc

There are a number of sizes of discs to choose from, each designed for optimum performance with the specific

Animation unit in action.

size of AMU backplate and the physical dimensions of the profile with which it is used. There are 12 designs to play with such as trangential, spiral, radial, linear etc (see reference chart in chapter 13), all of which have different directional and rhythmic effects on the 'movement' pattern of the gobo to be animated. The amount of gobo designs/disc designs available, and thus the innumerable potential combinations, means there is no substitute for experiment, whilst different lanterns can also give different results.

How to do it

Experimentation is key to obtaining successful results since the quality of the effect can be altered by a number of variables:

> **Choice of gobo**
> **Focus – balance between hard and soft**
> **Disc Pattern**
> **Direction and Orientation of disc movement**
> **Speed**
> **Colour**

1 Choose your gobo

Choose the gobo image you wish to animate, e.g. water, cloud, fire. NB: This does not always have to be the most obvious design – see the examples below where cloud designs have been used to create a wealth of different effects. Load your gobo into the gobo gate in the normal way.

2 Focus

NB: A gobo in hard focus will not wiggle! Animation capabilities can only be fully explored by putting the gobo out of focus to a greater or lesser degree, depending on the result required. By putting the gobo off-focus, you are utilising the less efficient part of the lantern optics which will then create an impression of movement.

3 Choose the orientation of the disc

The animation disc can be 'top' or 'side' mounted: top mounting (when the motor housing is above the colour frame) gives a side to side movement suitable for clouds and flowing water; side mounting (when the motor housing is to the side of the colour frame) gives a vertical movement useful for water ripples, rising flames or heat haze.

4. Choose the direction of disc

Direction of movement can be reversed either by the controller or by a switch on the AMU motor housing. It is also worth noting that the direction of movement alters on either side of hard focus and gives further subtle variations.

5 Speed
Animation unit speeds are slower than rotators, ranging from 0-6rpm, as effects tend to require slower speeds.

6 Colour
Colour can be added to the colour frame in the normal fashion but is especially effective if stuck onto the animation disc itself in strips of different hues. This lends much more variation to the overall effect.

In Chapter 13 there is a reference chart which gives examples of disc and gobo combinations to create popular effects such as a passing train and water ripples, etc.

Hints and Tips
Below are some examples of effects based around the principles of introducing minor alterations in gobo design, disc design, speed, focus, orientation and colour. Obviously the printed page curtails the effect so you will have to try it yourself! Experimentation will reveal how many different effects can be achieved with just a few basic tools.

Try experimenting with some of the following:

Furious Flames
Try cloud gobo 448 (Distorted Cloud) … and a very fast AMU disc 18 to give a dramatic raging fire with the addition of split gels of red, orange and yellow.

This unorthodox choice of gobo creates an unexpected result – give it a softer focus to create the impression of smoky, furious flames. Use the same combination again with the gobo in a conventional, horizontal, orientation, a slower speed on the AMU and paler colours and you can change

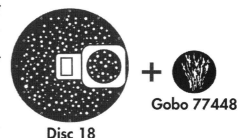

Disc 18

Gobo 77448

Furious flames: AMU Disc 18 with Distorted Cloud gobo (vertical).

the effect to distant undulating clouds. Increase the speed and you can change the effect from a gentle breeze to a real twister! Small changes to the orientation, speed and colour can have hugely varied effects.

Flame Effect
Move this reflected water gobo through 90° and add a red/orange gel added to create a flame effect. This shows how you do not have to stick to the description of the gobo to get a particular effect.

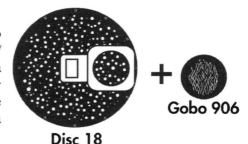

Disc 18

Flame effect: AMU Disc 18 with Reflected Water gobo 906 (vertical).

Rippling Water
The same gobo could be used in horizontal orientation, with blue gels and an AMU 12 at a slower speed to create gently rippling water.

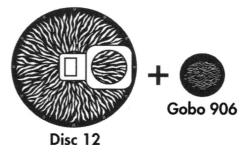

Disc 12

Rippling water: AMU Disc 12 with Reflected Water gobo 906 (horizontal).

Lava Flow
Use Cloud gobo 168 with red/orange split gels and AMU disc 18. Don't be bound by the conventional – experiment and be inventive. Something as simple as altering the focus or the direction of movement on the disc would change this from a lava flow to a heat haze or even steam!

Disc 18

Lava flow: AMU Disc 18 with Cloud gobo 168.

A cloud effect with no gobo!
Just a split gel and an AMU disc 18 at slow speed gives the effect of clouds in continuous motion.

You don't always need a gobo. Sometimes just the interaction of disc and colour is enough.

It is also possible to put certain animation discs on non-profile lanterns. Some AMU discs [DHA 20, 21 & 22, Rosco 30020, 30021, 30022] have been designed precisely for this purpose.

Non-profile lantern discs.

Traditional theatre lighting effects are being used more and more in the architectural environment. They help to make a shopping trip or visit to a museum or restaurant a much more entertaining occasion – rather like an extension of a visit to the theatre it lends drama and interest. People can eat, shop, meet in a carefully enhanced atmosphere

These white units were installed in a shopping mall in Hong Kong by Pacific Lighting (HK) Ltd. The effect was designed to create a calming gentle undulation of light as the shoppers entered the mall, in keeping with the cool stylish décor of the mall and to encourage shoppers to linger.

The mood of an installation can be altered by, for example, projecting flames onto a

A white animation unit and disc on a white ETC Source 4 Profile. Ho Man Tin Shopping Mall for the Hong Kong Housing Authority. Courtesy of Pacific Lighting HK Ltd.

featureless blank wall (to create a feeling of warmth rather than evacuate the building!). Lighting can be altered to suit seasons e.g. using snow flakes in winter, falling leaves in autumn or even rain!

The only limit is your imagination!

Double Gate Animation

Double gate animation is a refinement of the animated gobo where a second gobo is added, in a specially adapted gobo holder, into the effects gate of the profile. The combination of gobos might be, for example, a window and tree branches. By hard focusing the window gobo, the tree branches are necessarily put into soft focus by the short focal plane of the lantern. With the addition of an animation unit it is possible to obtain the impression of movement in the off-focus gobo – in this case the tree branches – without animating the window frame. Thus the impression of tree branches waving outside the window can be created.

Hints and Tips

Make sure you get the correct image in hard focus or you may find your window frame blowing in the breeze while the tree stays still!

Rotator Animation

For some effects it is also possible to create a rudimentary animation effect using a gobo rotator. For example, a softly focused fire effect gobo can be placed in the gobo slot whilst a spiral gobo can be placed in a gobo rotator. The spiral is also placed off-focus and the gobo rotator, moving slowly, can animate the fire gobo with the spiral's movement.

Be warned however that this is not suitable for all applications as the rotational motion can be quite evident.

Other Gobo Gizmos

GAM Film/FX

GAM Film/FX has a continuous loop of etched stainless steel or polyester film which passes through the gate of a profile to create animated effects. Motion is more linear than the cyclic animation disc but the result is a matter of preference and depends on the type of effect you want to achieve. Film loops can be off the shelf or customised to your own design and snap into the unit. Control can be either variable speed or mains operated for full speed operation.

The original unit has a loop life of approximately 100 hours so is not recommended for continuous use in display and theme park applications and is better suited for theatre use. For longer periods an SX4 model can be used which claims a loop life of 2,000 to 4,000 hours.

The SX4 system also offers a gobo changer accessory for an ETC Source 4, with options for either a six-way M size or four-way B size gobo changer.

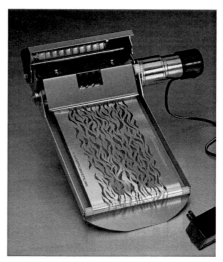

GAM Film Effects.

White Light/City Theatrical VSFX/VSFX3 units

A development from the animation unit is the White Light VSFX unit which dispenses with the gobo altogether and adopts a large glass disc with a photographic image adhered to its surface to create water ripples, flames, rain and snow effects.

A different form of projected animation can be seen in the GAM Film/FX.

White Light/City Theatrical VSFX3 unit .

Patrick Woodroffe
Lighting Designer, UK: Music, Dance, Fashion, Art and Architecture

Gobos make life easy – too easy sometimes! The ability to texture a theatrical scene and give it a sense of time and place, to give it some sort of credence, is magical and instantaneous.

When the first moving light programmers turned the lights into the audience at a rock show, it must have been some sort of eureka moment. And then when they started to rotate the gobos, perhaps simply to index them, and discovered that beautiful effect with which we are all now so familiar, it must have been an extraordinary experience.

REFERENCE

Mr Motoi Hattori
Lighting Designer, Japan: Opera, Drama, Musical.

Sunlight and moonlight filtering through the trees, or a bright beam cutting through the mist and fog are truly beautiful sights. When I try to express this beauty on stage I use a Gobo spotlight, further emphasising the existing light while simultaneously conveying shadows and depth. The reverse is also true, when the resulting light from Gobos is so subtle that the audience becomes absorbed in the performance. It is always a pleasure to select which Gobo I will be working with for my next stage design.

Katharine Williams
Lighting Designer, UK: Drama, Dance, Physical Theatre, Opera, Musical, Circus

The most exciting development in the dance and circus work I light is the new glass gobo technology. This allows me to choose, or custom design, gobos that tie the lighting completely into the projection to create a single visual world in which you can't see where one element ends and the other begins. Using a mixture of tungsten and non-tungsten fixtures helps to create a depth of lighting texture, but it is the gobos that really do the work, linking all the components of the design by allowing the beams of light to have the same flavour, whether from a generic profile, a moving head profile or from a projector.

12 GOBO FAMILIES AND EXAMPLES

Several gobo makers have more than 1000 image designs available in several sizes: many are similar, but few, if any are identical.

These images can be found in the company catalogues, on posters and their websites, and in several cases as Apps on the iphone.

We have divided the thousands of images into design families, and show designs from some companies to illustrate the diversity These companies are:

Rosco DHA
Apollo Design Technologies
Goboland
Projected Image
Great American Market
Lee Filters
PRG

All images shown here are the property of the companies listed and are copyright.

BREAKUPS

77879
Triangle Breakup
Rosco/DHA

79076
Triangles 2
Rosco/DHA

726
Smash
GAM

79650
Bubbles (small)
Rosco/DHA

611
Crackling Breakup
GAM

78444
Diamond Sphere
Rosco/DHA

79662
Linear 9
Rosco/DHA

77401
Linear 1
Rosco/DHA

77421
Wrectilinear
Rosco/DHA

77432
Spellbound
Rosco/DHA

398
Shatter
GAM

77721
Breakup (Small)
Rosco/DHA

77915
Foam
Rosco/DHA

880
Bursting Breakup
GAM

78445
Grid Sphere
Rosco/DHA

78048
Weave
Rosco/DHA

136 Gobos for Image Projection

77809
Sharp Breakup (small)
Rosco/DHA

77280
Jaws 1
Rosco/DHA

271
Radial Breakup
GAM

77217
Pick Up Sticks Reversed
Rosco/DHA

77420
Rectilinear
Rosco/DHA

77956
Camouflage (brown)
Rosco/DHA

77957
Camouflage (green)
Rosco/DHA

77575
Reflected Bubbles
Rosco/DHA

669
Shimmer
GAM

659
Bark 4
Projected Image

2 270 050
Abstract Breakup
Goboland

2 230 052
Random Square 2
Goboland

2 240 004
Metal Grid 2
Goboland

2 270 021
Wood Grain
Goboland

2 270 002
Inverted Marble
Goboland

MS-2167
Bean Breakup
Apollo

Gobos for Image Projection 137

FOLIAGE BREAKUPS

77805
Leaf Breakup (medium)
Rosco/DHA

77406
Dapple (medium)
Rosco/DHA

79106
Leafy Branches
Rosco/DHA

351
Saplings
GAM

77840
Meshed Woodlands
Rosco/DHA

77774
Blossoms
Rosco/DHA

77730
Palm
Rosco/DHA

622
Maple Vines
Projected Image

77732
Realistic Leaves
Rosco/DHA

77107
Pine Branches
Rosco/DHA

GB 260 020
Tropical Leaf
Lee Filters

2 260 000
Bamboozle
Goboland

2 260 030
Oak Leaves
Goboland

2 260 006
Beech Leaves Medium
Goboland

MS-1084
Breakup Hemp
Apollo

MS-3590
Fancy Leaves
Apollo

TREES & FLOWERS

77777
Bare Branches 2
Rosco/DHA

77838
Palm Tree
Rosco/DHA

77100
Tree 2
Rosco/DHA

77860
Glade
Rosco/DHA

681
Baobab Tree
Projected Image

253
Rose
GAM

78434
Tree Silhouette 3
Rosco/DHA

77863
Branching Leaves (pos)
Rosco/DHA

77864
Branching Leaves (neg)
Rosco/DHA

71059
Wheat
Rosco/DHA

71055
Sunburst Flowers
Rosco/DHA

GB 260 049
Barley
Lee Filters

2 260 051
Japanese Bamboo (take)
Goboland

2 260 054
Japanese Grasses 2
Goboland

MS-3572
Slender Forest
Apollo

MS-3540
Trees Oak Forest (Rev)
Apollo

ABSTRACT

77528
Eastern Lattice
Rosco/DHA

77746
Colorswap Lattice
Rosco/DHA

532
Foundation
GAM

960
Big Sharp
Projected Image

77753
Lashes
Rosco/DHA

77441
Saigon Roofs 2
Rosco/DHA

77783
Antique Rosette
Rosco/DHA

77395
Geometrics 5
Rosco/DHA

2 210 010
Regular Web
Goboland

2 200 041
Grid Warp 1
Goboland

GB 420 004
Explosion
Lee Filters

2 270 062
Abstract Floral
Goboland

2 270 010
Ocelot Markings
Goboland

2 170 005
Dot Pattern 3
Goboland

MS 2183
Metal Truss Breakup 2
Apollo

MS 2202
Beams 2
Apollo

140 Gobos for Image Projection

77565
Flying Shapes 1
Rosco/DHA

78135
Splash
Rosco/DHA

455
Furry Bar
Projected Image

77439
Compass Rose
Rosco/DHA

76549
Good Luck
Rosco/DHA

78470
Puzzled
Rosco/DHA

78471
Puzzled Reversed
Rosco/DHA

390
Austrian Curtain
GAM

78049
Chessboard
Rosco/DHA

332
Transom
GAM

78046
Perspective Lines 1
Rosco/DHA

77620
Moire Lines
Rosco/DHA

78053
Perspective Chessboard
Rosco/DHA

471
Linear 12
Projected Image

1073
Curly Swirl
Projected Image

758
Archers Arrow
Projected Image

77392
Geometrics 2
Rosco/DHA

77393
Geometrics 3
Rosco/DHA

77761
Spiral
Rosco/DHA

79054
Catherine Wheel
Rosco/DHA

77427
Pinwheel
Rosco/DHA

77897
Hangover
Rosco/DHA

1015
Contours
Projected Image

77426
Cone & Spot
Rosco/DHA

371
3 Offset Rings
Projected Image

78247
Spun Dots Large
Rosco/DHA

77921
Hour Hand
Rosco/DHA

71037
Lines 1
Rosco/DHA

372
4 Offset Rings
Projected Image

78474
Contrast
Rosco/DHA

74010
Symmetric 10
Rosco/DHA

329
Atom
GAM

78073
Circles 1
Rosco/DHA

2 220 016
Radar Swoop
Goboland

2 210 015
Vector Tunnel
Goboland

2 221 013
Spiral
Goboland

2 221 021
Ammonite Spiral 1
Goboland

2 221 026
Tunnel Warp 2
Goboland

2 221 031
Squirlpool
Goboland

2 170 001
Spot on 100%
Goboland

GB 170 011
Spot Line 1
Lee Filters

GB 220 028
Crystal
Lee Filters

2 220 017
Radar Radial Swoop
Goboland

2 221 028
Rose Spiral
Goboland

MS 1006
Swirl Stairway
Apollo

MS 2264
Stir The Pot
Apollo

MS 2271
Twister
Apollo

MS 2470
Pinwheel
Apollo

6032
Businessman
Projected Image

78076
Woman
Rosco/DHA

77964
Single Cross
Rosco/DHA

77971
Entrance/Exit
Rosco/DHA

5016
Camera
Projected Image

77688
Walk This Way
Rosco/DHA

77678
First Aid
Rosco/DHA

77690
Welcome
Rosco/DHA

77680
Information
Rosco/DHA

77689
Sale
Rosco/DHA

2 500 000
Stage Door
Goboland

2 540 006
All Toilets
Goboland

GB 541 016
Skull and Crossbones
Lee Filters

GB 540 015
No Entry
Lee Filters

GB 540 014
Casino
Lee Filters

MS 6040
City Building Lights
Apollo

77946
Japan
Rosco/DHA

777876
Europe
Rosco/DHA

77821
Istanbul
Rosco/DHA

77820
Paris
Rosco/DHA

77975
Sydney
Rosco/DHA

77309
Broadway 2
Rosco/DHA

3026
Angel of the North
Projected Image

77213
Fairy Castle
Rosco/DHA

77741
Fire Escapes
Rosco/DHA

78113
Hollywood
Rosco/DHA

78145
Pyramids
Rosco/DHA

237
American Flag
GAM

GB 551 001
Statue of Liberty
Lee Filters

2 553 000
Tower of Pisa
Goboland

GB 554 010
Stonehenge
Lee Filters

GB 510 060
Red Square
Lee Filters

77856
York Minster
Rosco/DHA

77207
Heraldics 6
Rosco/DHA

77845
Medieval
Rosco/DHA

77802
Stained Glass Complete
Rosco/DHA

78521
Clasped Hands
Rosco/DHA

2 520 002
Celtic 2
Goboland

2 520 008
Celtic 8
Goboland

77537
Stained Glass
Rosco/DHA

BOUNDARIES & WILDLIFE

78538
Cranes
Rosco/DHA

78033
Picket Fence
Rosco/DHA

77519
Stone Wall
Rosco/DHA

77527
Bricks
Rosco/DHA

77787
Cobblestones
Rosco/DHA

GB 502 009
Barbed Wire
Lee Filters

77130
Half Web
Rosco/DHA

78090
Moth
Rosco/DHA

WINDOWS, DOORS & BLINDS

77703
Double Hung Window
Rosco/DHA

77142
Georgian
Rosco/DHA

77644
Georgian Shadow
Rosco/DHA

77702
Venetian Blind
Rosco/DHA

77904
Venetian Blind 2
Rosco/DHA

77337
Eastern
Rosco/DHA

77645
Venetian Shadow
Rosco/DHA

586
Grid
GAM

77138
"Cats" Window
Rosco/DHA

77139
Venetian
Rosco/DHA

76568
Classic Door
Rosco/DHA

2 480 015
Window 15
Goboland

GB 470 004
Church 2
Lee Filters

2 480 007
Window 7
Goboland

2 490 008
Blinds 8
Goboland

MS 6031
Door Closed
Apollo

CLOUDS

77165
Cloud 7
Rosco/DHA

77168
Cloud 10
Rosco/DHA

77610
Strato-Cumulus
Rosco/DHA

78170
Cloud Outlines
Rosco/DHA

77163
Cloud 5
Rosco/DHA

78241
Layered Cloud
Rosco/DHA

226
Cloud 3
GAM

266
Sunburst
GAM

SKY

77932
Stars 6
Rosco/DHA

79004
Saturn
Rosco/DHA

77220
Moon
Rosco/DHA

77850
Shooting Stars
Rosco/DHA

2 120 014
Dappled Cloud Small
Goboland

GB 120 010
Storm
Lee Filters

2 120 015
Dappled Cloud Medium
Goboland

MS 1131
Sun
Apollo

WATER

77903
Reflected Water 1
Rosco/DHA

77958
Water 4
Rosco/DHA

77989
"Les Mis" Whirlpool
Rosco/DHA

594
Splash
GAM

2 300 001
Waves 1
Goboland

GB 300 020
Waterfall
Lee Filters

GB 300 023
Fountain
Lee Filters

MS 1032
Water Shimmering
Apollo

FIRE & ICE

77177
Lightning 2
Rosco/DHA

2 130 002
Fine Rain 2
Goboland

77884
Snow
Rosco/DHA

533
Snowflake B-Up 3
Projected Image

77771
Snowflake
Rosco/DHA

77175
Flames 1
Rosco/DHA

79172
Flames 6
Rosco/DHA

2 130 025
Lightning 1
Goboland

78369
Bells 1
Rosco/DHA

77720
Santa and Sleigh
Rosco/DHA

335
Clown (V)
GAM

78007
Candles/Menorah
Rosco/DHA

5002
Vintage Racer
Projected Image

77766
Fireworks 1
Rosco/DHA

77234
Witch
Rosco/DHA

4023
Angel
Projected Image

77650
Kung Hay Fat Choi
Rosco/DHA

79143
Cafe Bar
Rosco/DHA

71061
Happy Anniversary
Rosco/DHA

77303
Balloons
Rosco/DHA

2 450 002
Tragicomedy 2
Goboland

GB 431 000
Love
Lee Filters

2 431 015
I Love You
Goboland

GB 421 007
Lucky Horseshoe
Lee Filters

B/W GLASS - ABSTRACT & BREAKUPS

425
Cube Pattern
Projected Image

82221
Infinity
Rosco/DHA

0924
Speckles
PRG

82755
Bounce
Rosco/DHA

82718
Cluster
Rosco/DHA

155
Constructed
Projected Image

81132
Atoms
Rosco/DHA

0801
Mesh Fence BU
PRG

82201
Whirlpool
Rosco/DHA

0920
Grass Break up
PRG

0679
Hex Break up
PRG

2001
Real Tree Bark 1
PRG

82713
Fractal 2
Rosco/DHA

0110
Single Shutter
PRG

82765
Circulate
Rosco/DHA

82724
Star Fusion
Rosco/DHA

B/W GLASS - ROTATION

82213
Gyroscope
Rosco/DHA

0685
Expanded Lines
PRG

81103
45° Shear Polar
Rosco/DHA

82704
Ricochet
Rosco/DHA

0682
Bloated Dots
PRG

0701
Crackle Linear Small
PRG

82719
Shimmer
Rosco/DHA

0073
Joined Rings 3
PRG

B/W GLASS - SCENE

81174
Full
Rosco/DHA

0610
City Skyline London
PRG

81185
Perfect Cloud
Rosco/DHA

0764
Reflected Water 1
PRG

0500
Osterley Foliage
PRG

82734
Cityscape 2
Rosco/DHA

1007015
Saturn 2
Goboland

1009005
Grass
Goboland

COLOURED GLASS - ABSTRACT & BREAKUPS

86745
Strung Theory
Rosco/DHA

86629
Emosphere Cyan
Rosco/DHA

86601
Color Weave
Rosco/DHA

86623
Hocus
Rosco/DHA

86608
Bubbles
Rosco/DHA

86622
Color Wave
Rosco/DHA

1010006
Pyromaniac
Goboland

CS 0107
Blurred Edges
Apollo

COLOURED GLASS - ROTATION

84421
Color Twist
Rosco/DHA

86605
45° Shear Polar
Rosco/DHA

86644
Spiral Bling
Rosco/DHA

86656
Harlequin Aperture
Rosco/DHA

1011002
All Dizzy
Goboland

86661
Aqua Marble
Rosco/DHA

062
Orango
Projected Image

CS 0091
Swirl Soft
Apollo

COLOURED GLASS - SCENE

86680
St Malo
Rosco/DHA

86675
Comedia
Rosco/DHA

86682
Epiphany
Rosco/DHA

86714
Beauty's Rainbow
Rosco/DHA

1010016
Blue Planet
Goboland

501
Cloudy Sky Colour 1
Projected Image

7107
Blue Ice
Projected Image

CS 0109
Meadow
Apollo

Tanya Burns
Lighting Designer, UK: Architectural, Exhibition.

Gobos are not my favourite thing, but they do have their place in the lighting designer's palette. My preference is to use them sparingly as a means of creating perspective depth by layering gobos and adding subtle movement. With the correct angles, this can generate visual interest in what might otherwise be a fairly flat, two-dimensional view of a space-restricted set.

Another approach is to use them unapologetically with bold, striking shapes to completely transform an environment. Of course, this is totally dependent on the style of production in which you are involved.

13 ANIMATION UNIT REFERENCES AND EFFECTS EXAMPLES

A selection of animation wheel designs for use in animating static gobo images and some popular effects combinations

Some popular effects combinations.

Disc 12
either orientation
very slow/slow rotation

Reflected water: Disc 12 mounted horizontally with Gobo 903 or 906.

Disc 13
either orientation
slow/medium rotation

Blowing flames:Disc 13 mounted vertically with Gobo 175 or 176.

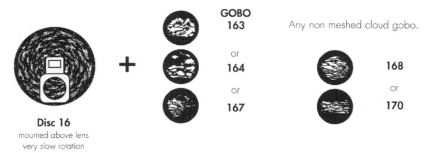

Disc 16
mounted above lens
very slow rotation

Clouds: Disc 16 mounted vertically with Gobo 163, 164, 167, 168 or 170.

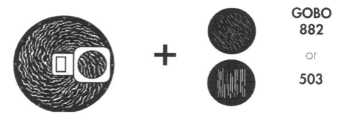

**GOBO
882**

or

503

Disc 13
mounted beside lens
medium rotation

Rain: Disc 13 mounted horizontally with Gobo 882 or 503.

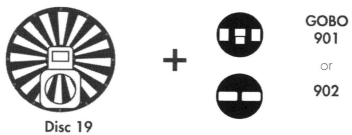

**GOBO
901**

or

902

Disc 19
mounted above lens
fast rotation

*Passing Train: Disc 19 mounted vertically with Gobo 901 or 902. NB Blanking out
some spaces in the disc will create a pulsing effect which emulates the space between
passing carriages.*

Footnote:

It is worth mentioning that there are a number of gobo manufacturers worldwide who produce ranges of catalogue gobos and/or custom gobos, along with the accessories that go with them. Many of these manufacturers also offer very useful product sheets and downloads which explain and elucidate their products, and range from catalogue designs to how to get the best from your gobo gizmos. They are certainly worth looking at.

Some excellent websites include:

Rosco Laboratories Inc & London: www.rosco.com
DHA Lighting (now part of Rosco): www.dhalighting.com
Apollo Design Technologies: www.internetapollo.com
Goboland: www.goboland.com
Projected Image: www.projectedimage.com
Great American Market: www.gamonline.com
Beacon Gobo Group: www.gobogroup.com
Lee Filters: www.leefilters.com

Gavan Swift
Lighting Designer, Australia: Plays, Musicals, Corporate Events.

I guess I'm partial to using linear break-ups as sidelight on performers. Whether in musicals or in plays, the irregular linear patterns of gobos such as 77501 Linear 3 and 77504 Linear 6 create a very dramatic, broken-up quality of light without looking like an obvious gobo. They even work well when sharp focussed, then softened with some R132 Medium Blue filter. If I feel the production needs some moody, dappled light, I tend to use R77780 Dense Leaves (Detail). This gobo lets through enough light that will illuminate performers without being obviously recognisable as a foliage gobo. It also joins together on the deck quite well and looks very striking with a little haze.

CONTRIBUTING LIGHTING DESIGNERS

PEOPLE INDEX

ENTERTAINMENT TECHNOLOGY PRESS

FREE SUBSCRIPTION SERVICE

Keeping Up To Date with

Gobos for Image Projection

Entertainment Technology titles are continually up-dated, and all major changes and additions are listed in date order in the relevant dedicated area of the publisher's website. Simply go to the front page of www.etnow.com and click on the BOOKS button. From there you can locate the title and be connected through to the latest information and services related to the publication.

The content of this book is correct at the time of publishing, to the best of the authors' knowledge. We welcome suggestions and comments for future editions of the book, which should be addressed to roscomh@aol.com or julie@joolzharper.co.uk

Titles Published by Entertainment Technology Press

ABC of Theatre Jargon *Francis Reid* **£9.95** ISBN 1904031099
This glossary of theatrical terminology explains the common words and phrases that are used in normal conversation between actors, directors, designers, technicians and managers.

Aluminium Structures in the Entertainment Industry *Peter Hind* **£24.95**
ISBN 1904031064
Aluminium Structures in the Entertainment Industry aims to educate the reader in all aspects of the design and safe usage of temporary and permanent aluminium structures specific to the entertainment industry – such as roof structures, PA towers, temporary staging, etc.

AutoCAD 2010 – A Handbook for Theatre Users *David Ripley* **£24.95** ISBN 9781904031611
From 'Setting Up' to 'Drawing in Three Dimensions' via 'Drawings Within Drawings', this compact and fully illustrated guide to AutoCAD covers everything from the basics to full colour rendering and remote plotting. Title completely revised in June 2010.

Automation in the Entertainment Industry – A User's Guide *Mark Ager and John Hastie* **£29.95** ISBN 9781904031581
In the last 15 years, there has been a massive growth in the use of automation in entertainment, especially in theatres, and it is now recognised as its own discipline. However, it is still only used in around 5% of theatres worldwide. In the next 25 years, given current growth patterns, that figure will rise to 30%. This will mean that the majority of theatre personnel, including directors, designers, technical staff, actors and theatre management, will come into contact with automation for the first time at some point in their careers. This book is intended to provide insights and practical advice from those who use automation, to help the first-time user understand the issues and avoid the pitfalls in its implementation. In the past, theatre automation was seen by many as a complex, unreliable and expensive toy, not for general use. The aim of this book is to dispel that myth.

Basics – A Beginner's Guide to Lighting Design *Peter Coleman* **£9.95** ISBN 1904031412
The fourth in the author's 'Basics' series, this title covers the subject area in four main sections: The Concept, Practical Matters, Related Issues and The Design Into Practice. In an area that is difficult to be definitive, there are several things that cross all the boundaries of all lighting design and it's these areas that the author seeks to help with.

Basics – A Beginner's Guide to Special Effects *Peter Coleman* **£9.95** ISBN 1904031331
This title introduces newcomers to the world of special effects. It describes all types of special effects including pyrotechnic, smoke and lighting effects, projections, noise machines, etc. It places emphasis on the safe storage, handling and use of pyrotechnics.

Basics – A Beginner's Guide to Stage Lighting *Peter Coleman* **£9.95** ISBN 190403120X
This title does what it says: it introduces newcomers to the world of stage lighting. It will not teach the reader the art of lighting design, but will teach beginners much about the 'nuts and bolts' of stage lighting.

Basics: A Beginner's Guide to Stage Management *Peter Coleman* **£7.95**
ISBN 9781904031475
The fifth in Peter Coleman's popular 'Basics' series, this title provides a practical insight into, and the definition of, the role of stage management. Further chapters describe Cueing or 'Calling' the Show (the Prompt Book), and the Hardware and Training for Stage Management. This is a book about people and systems, without which most of the technical equipment used by others in the performance workplace couldn't function.

Basics – A Beginner's Guide to Stage Sound *Peter Coleman* **£9.95** ISBN 1904031277
This title does what it says: it introduces newcomers to the world of stage sound. It will not teach the reader the art of sound design, but will teach beginners much about the background to sound reproduction in a theatrical environment.

Building Better Theaters *Michael Mell* **£16.95** 1904031404
A title within our Consultancy Series, this book describes the process of designing a theater, from the initial decision to build through to opening night. Michael Mell's book provides a step-by-step guide to the design and construction of performing arts facilities. Chapters discuss: assembling your team, selecting an architect, different construction methods, the architectural design process, construction of the theater, theatrical systems and equipment, the stage, backstage, the auditorium, ADA requirements and the lobby. Each chapter clearly describes what to expect and how to avoid surprises. It is a must-read for architects, planners, performing arts groups, educators and anyone who may be considering building or renovating a theater.

Case Studies in Crowd Management
Chris Kemp, Iain Hill, Mick Upton, Mark Hamilton **£16.95** ISBN 9781904031482
This important work has been compiled from a series of research projects carried out by the staff of the Centre for Crowd Management and Security Studies at Buckinghamshire Chilterns University College, and seminar work carried out in Berlin and Groningen with partner Yourope. It includes case studies, reports and a crowd management safety plan for a major outdoor rock concert, safe management of rock concerts utilising a triple barrier safety system and pan-European Health & Safety Issues.

Close Protection – The Softer Skills *Geoffrey Padgham* **£11.95** ISBN 1904031390
This is the first educational book in a new 'Security Series' for Entertainment Technology Press, and it coincides with the launch of the new 'Protective Security Management' Foundation Degree at Buckinghamshire Chilterns University College (BCUC). The author is a former full-career Metropolitan Police Inspector from New Scotland Yard with 27 years' experience of close protection (CP). For 22 of those years he specialised in operations and senior management duties with the Royalty Protection Department at Buckingham Palace, followed by five years in the private security industry specialising in CP training design and delivery. His wealth of protection experience comes across throughout the text, which incorporates sound advice and exceptional practical guidance, subtly separating fact from fiction. This publication is an excellent form of reference material for experienced operatives, students and trainees.

A Comparative Study of Crowd Behaviour at Two Major Music Events
Chris Kemp, Iain Hill, Mick Upton **£7.95** ISBN 1904031250
A compilation of the findings of reports made at two major live music concerts, and in particular crowd behaviour, which is followed from ingress to egress.

Control Freak *Wayne Howell* **£28.95** ISBN 9781904031550
Control Freak is the second book by Wayne Howell. It provides an in depth study of DMX512 and the new RDM (Remote Device Management) standards. The book is aimed at both users and developers and provides a wealth of real world information based on the author's twenty year experience of lighting control.

Copenhagen Opera House *Richard Brett and John Offord* **£32.00** ISBN 1904031420
Completed in a little over three years, the Copenhagen Opera House opened with a royal gala performance on 15th January 2005. Built on a spacious brown-field site, the building is a landmark venue and this book provides the complete technical background story to an opera house set to become a benchmark for future design and planning. Sixteen chapters by relevant experts involved with the project cover everything from the planning of the auditorium and studio stage, the stage engineering, stage lighting and control and architectural lighting through to acoustic design and sound technology plus technical summaries.

Electrical Safety for Live Events *Marco van Beek* **£16.95** ISBN 1904031285
This title covers electrical safety regulations and good pracitise pertinent to the entertainment industries and includes some basic electrical theory as well as clarifying the "do's and don't's" of working with electricity.

Entertainment in Production Volume 1: 1994-1999 *Rob Halliday* **£24.95**
ISBN 9781904031512

Entertainment in Production Volume 2: 2000-2006 *Rob Halliday* **£24.95**
ISBN 9781904031529
Rob Halliday has a dual career as a lighting designer/programmer and author and in these two volumes he provides the intriguing but comprehensive technical background stories behind the major musical productions and other notable projects spanning the period 1994 to 2005. Having been closely involved with the majority of the events described, the author is able to present a first-hand and all-encompassing portrayal of how many of the major shows across the past decade came into being. From *Oliver!* and *Miss Saigon* to *Mamma Mia!* and *Mary Poppins*, here the complete technical story unfolds. The books, which are profusely illustrated, are in large part an adapted selection of articles that first appeared in the magazine *Lighting&Sound International*.

Entertainment Technology Yearbook 2008 *John Offord* **£14.95** ISBN 9781904031543
The new Entertainment Technology Yearbook 2008 covers the year 2007 and includes picture coverage of major industry exhibitions in Europe compiled from the pages of Entertainment Technology magazine and the etnow.com website, plus articles and pictures of production, equipment and project highlights of the year. Also included is a major European Trade Directory that will be regularly updated on line. A new edition will be published each year at the ABTT Theatre Show in London in June.

The Exeter Theatre Fire *David Anderson* **£24.95** ISBN 1904031137
This title is a fascinating insight into the events that led up to the disaster at the Theatre Royal, Exeter, on the night of September 5th 1887. The book details what went wrong, and the lessons that were learned from the event.

Fading Light – A Year in Retirement *Francis Reid* **£14.95** ISBN 1904031358
Francis Reid, the lighting industry's favourite author, describes a full year in retirement. "Old

age is much more fun than I expected," he says. Fading Light describes visits and experiences to the author's favourite theatres and opera houses, places of relaxation and re-visits to scholarly institutions.

Focus on Lighting Technology *Richard Cadena* **£17.95** ISBN 1904031145
This concise work unravels the mechanics behind modern performance lighting and appeals to designers and technicians alike. Packed with clear, easy-to-read diagrams, the book provides excellent explanations behind the technology of performance lighting.

The Followspot Guide *Nick Mobsby* **£28.95** ISBN 9781904031499
The first in ETP's Equipment Series, Nick Mobsby's Followspot Guide tells you everything you need to know about followspots, from their history through to maintenance and usage. It's pages include a technical specification of 193 followspots from historical to the latest 2007 versions from major manufacturers.

From Ancient Rome to Rock 'n' Roll – a Review of the UK Leisure Security Industry *Mick Upton* **£14.95** ISBN 9781904031505
From stewarding, close protection and crowd management through to his engagement as a senior consultant Mick Upton has been ever present in the events industry. A founder of ShowSec International in 1982 he was its chairman until 2000. The author has led the way on training within the sector. He set up the ShowSec Training Centre and has acted as a consultant at the Bramshill Police College. He has been prominent in the development of courses at Buckinghamshire New University where he was awarded a Doctorate in 2005. Mick has received numerous industry awards. His book is a personal account of the development and professionalism of the sector across the past 50 years.

Health and Safety Aspects in the Live Music Industry *Chris Kemp, Iain Hill* **£30.00** ISBN 1904031226
This title includes chapters on various safety aspects of live event production and is written by specialists in their particular areas of expertise.

Health and Safety Management in the Live Music and Events Industry *Chris Hannam* **£25.95** ISBN 1904031307
This title covers the health and safety regulations and their application regarding all aspects of staging live entertainment events, and is an invaluable manual for production managers and event organisers.

Hearing the Light – 50 Years Backstage *Francis Reid* **£24.95** ISBN 1904031188
This highly enjoyable memoir delves deeply into the theatricality of the industry. The author's almost fanatical interest in opera, his formative period as lighting designer at Glyndebourne and his experiences as a theatre administrator, writer and teacher make for a broad and unique background.

An Introduction to Rigging in the Entertainment Industry *Chris Higgs* **£24.95** ISBN 1904031129
This book is a practical guide to rigging techniques and practices and also thoroughly covers safety issues and discusses the implications of working within recommended guidelines and regulations. Second edition revised September 2008.

Let There be Light – Entertainment Lighting Software Pioneers in Conversation *Robert Bell* **£32.00** ISBN 1904031242
Robert Bell interviews a distinguished group of software engineers working on entertainment lighting ideas and products.

Light and Colour Filters *Michael Hall and Eddie Ruffell* **£23.95** ISBN 9781904031598
Written by two acknowledged and respected experts in the field, this book is destined to become the standard reference work on the subject. The title chronicles the development and use of colour filters and also describes how colour is perceived and how filters function. Up-to-date reference tables will help the practitioner make better and more specific choices of colour.

Lighting for Roméo and Juliette *John Offord* **£26.95** ISBN 1904031161
John Offord describes the making of the Vienna State Opera production from the lighting designer's viewpoint – from the point where director Jürgen Flimm made his decision not to use scenery or sets and simply employ the expertise of LD Patrick Woodroffe.

Lighting Systems for TV Studios *Nick Mobsby* **£45.00** ISBN 1904031005
Lighting Systems for TV Studios, now in its second edition, is the first book specifically written on the subject and has become the 'standard' resource work for studio planning and design covering the key elements of system design, luminaires, dimming, control, data networks and suspension systems as well as detailing the infrastructure items such as cyclorama, electrical and ventilation. Sensibly TV lighting principles are explained and some history on TV broadcasting, camera technology and the equipment is provided to help set the scene! The second edition includes applications for sine wave and distributed dimming, moving lights, Ethernet and new cool lamp technology.

Lighting Techniques for Theatre-in-the-Round *Jackie Staines* **£24.95** ISBN 1904031013
Lighting Techniques for Theatre-in-the-Round is a unique reference source for those working on lighting design for theatre-in-the-round for the first time. It is the first title to be published specifically on the subject, it also provides some anecdotes and ideas for more challenging shows, and attempts to blow away some of the myths surrounding lighting in this format.

Lighting the Stage *Francis Reid* **£14.95** ISBN 1904031080
Lighting the Stage discusses the human relationships involved in lighting design – both between people, and between these people and technology. The book is written from a highly personal viewpoint and its 'thinking aloud' approach is one that Francis Reid has used in his writings over the past 30 years.

Model National Standard Conditions *ABTT/DSA/LGLA* **£20.00** ISBN 1904031110
These *Model National Standard Conditions* covers operational matters and complement *The Technical Standards for Places of Entertainment*, which describes the physical requirements for building and maintaining entertainment premises.

Mr Phipps' Theatre *Mark Jones, John Pick* **£17.95** ISBN: 1904031382
Mark Jones and John Pick describe "The Sensational Story of Eastbourne's Royal Hippodrome" – formerly Eastbourne Theatre Royal. An intriguing narrative, the book sets the story against a unique social history of the town. Peter Longman, former director of The Theatres Trust, provides the Foreword.

Pages From Stages *Anthony Field* **£17.95** ISBN 1904031269
Anthony Field explores the changing style of theatres including interior design, exterior design, ticket and seat prices, and levels of service, while questioning whether the theatre still exists as a place of entertainment for regular theatre-goers.

Performing Arts Technical Training Handbook 2009/2010 *ed: John Offord* **£19.95** ISBN 9781904031604
Published in association with the ABTT (Association of British Theatre Technicians), this important Handbook includes fully detailed and indexed entries describing courses on backstage crafts offered by over 100 universities and colleges across the UK. A completely new research project, with accompanying website, the title also includes articles with advice for those considering a career 'behind the scenes', together with contact information and descriptions of the major organisations involved with industry training – plus details of companies offering training within their own premises. The Handbook will be kept in print, with a major revision annually.

Practical Dimming *Nick Mobsby* **£22.95** ISBN 19040313447
This important and easy to read title covers the history of electrical and electronic dimming, how dimmers work, current dimmer types from around the world, planning of a dimming system, looking at new sine wave dimming technology and distributed dimming. Integration of dimming into different performance venues as well as the necessary supporting electrical systems are fully detailed. Significant levels of information are provided on the many different forms and costs of potential solutions as well as how to plan specific solutions. Architectural dimming for the likes of hotels, museums and shopping centres is included. Practical Dimming is a companion book to Practical DMX and is designed for all involved in the use, operation and design of dimming systems.

Practical DMX *Nick Mobsby* **£16.95** ISBN 1904031368
In this highly topical and important title the author details the principles of DMX, how to plan a network, how to choose equipment and cables, with data on products from around the world, and how to install DMX networks for shows and on a permanently installed basis. The easy style of the book and the helpful fault finding tips, together with a review of different DMX testing devices provide an ideal companion for all lighting technicians and system designers. An introduction to Ethernet and Canbus networks are provided as well tips on analogue networks and protocol conversion. This title has been recently updated to include a new chapter on Remote Device Management that became an international standard in Summer 2006.

Practical Guide to Health and Safety in the Entertainment Industry
Marco van Beek **£14.95** ISBN 1904031048
This book is designed to provide a practical approach to Health and Safety within the Live Entertainment and Event industry. It gives industry-pertinent examples, and seeks to break down the myths surrounding Health and Safety.

Production Management *Joe Aveline* **£17.95** ISBN 1904031102
Joe Aveline's book is an in-depth guide to the role of the Production Manager, and includes real-life practical examples and 'Aveline's Fables' – anecdotes of his experiences with real messages behind them.

Rigging for Entertainment: Regulations and Practice *Chris Higgs* **£19.95**
ISBN 1904031218
Continuing where he left off with his highly successful *An Introduction to Rigging in the Entertainment Industry*, Chris Higgs' second title covers the regulations and use of equipment in greater detail.

Rock Solid Ethernet *Wayne Howell* **£24.95** ISBN 1904031293
Although aimed specifically at specifiers, installers and users of entertainment industry systems, this book will give the reader a thorough grounding in all aspects of computer networks, whatever industry they may work in. The inclusion of historical and technical 'sidebars' make for an enjoyable as well as informative read.

Sixty Years of Light Work *Fred Bentham* **£26.95** ISBN 1904031072
This title is an autobiography of one of the great names behind the development of modern stage lighting equipment and techniques.

Sound for the Stage *Patrick Finelli* **£24.95** ISBN 1904031153
Patrick Finelli's thorough manual covering all aspects of live and recorded sound for performance is a complete training course for anyone interested in working in the field of stage sound, and is a must for any student of sound.

Stage Automation *Anton Woodward* **£12.95** ISBN 9781904031567
The purpose of this book is to explain the stage automation techniques used in modern theatre to achieve some of the spectacular visual effects seen in recent years. The book is targeted at automation operators, production managers, theatre technicians, stage engineering machinery manufacturers and theatre engineering students. Topics are covered in sufficient detail to provide an insight into the thought processes that the stage automation engineer has to consider when designing a control system to control stage machinery in a modern theatre. The author has worked on many stage automation projects and developed the award-winning Impressario stage automation system.

Stage Lighting Design in Britain: The Emergence of the Lighting Designer, 1881-1950 *Nigel Morgan* **£17.95** ISBN 190403134X
This book sets out to ascertain the main course of events and the controlling factors that determined the emergence of the theatre lighting designer in Britain, starting with the introduction of incandescent electric light to the stage, and ending at the time of the first public lighting design credits around 1950. The book explores the practitioners, equipment, installations and techniques of lighting design.

Stage Lighting for Theatre Designers *Nigel Morgan* **£17.95** ISBN 1904031196
This is an updated second edition of Nigel Morgan's popular book for students of theatre design – outlining all the techniques of stage lighting design.

Technical Marketing Techniques *David Brooks, Andy Collier, Steve Norman* **£24.95**
ISBN 190403103X
Technical Marketing is a novel concept, recently defined and elaborated by the authors of this book, with business-to-business companies competing in fast developing technical product sectors.

Technical Standards for Places of Entertainment *ABTT/DSA* **£45.00**
ISBN 9781904031536
Technical Standards for Places of Entertainment details the necessary physical standards
required for entertainment venues. New A4 revised edition June 2008.

Theatre Engineering and Stage Machinery *Toshiro Ogawa* **£30.00**
ISBN 9781904031024
Theatre Engineering and Stage Machinery is a unique reference work covering every aspect
of theatrical machinery and stage technology in global terms, and across the complete
historical spectrum. Revised February 2007.

Theatre Lighting in the Age of Gas *Terence Rees* **£24.95** ISBN 190403117X
Entertainment Technology Press has republished this valuable historic work previously
produced by the Society for Theatre Research in 1978. *Theatre Lighting in the Age of Gas*
investigates the technological and artistic achievements of theatre lighting engineers from
the 1700s to the late Victorian period.

Theatre Space: A Rediscovery Reported *Francis Reid* **£19.95** ISBN 1904031439
In the post-war world of the 1950s and 60s, the format of theatre space became a matter for
a debate that aroused passions of an intensity unknown before or since. The proscenium
arch was clearly identified as the enemy, accused of forming a barrier to disrupt the relations
between the actor and audience. An uneasy fellow-traveller at the time, Francis Reid later
recorded his impressions whilst enjoying performances or working in theatres old and new
and this book is an important collection of his writings in various theatrical journals from
1969-2001 including his contribution to the Cambridge Guide to the Theatre in 1988. It
reports some of the flavour of the period when theatre architecture was rediscovering its past
in a search to establish its future.

Theatres of Achievement *John Higgins* **£29.95** ISBN: 1904031374
John Higgins affectionately describes the history of 40 distinguished UK theatres in a
personal tribute, each uniquely illustrated by the author. Completing each profile is colour
photography by Adrian Eggleston.

Theatric Tourist *Francis Reid* **£19.95** ISBN 9781904031468
Theatric Tourist is the delightful story of Francis Reid's visits across more than 50 years
to theatres, theatre museums, performances and even movie theme parks. In his inimi-
table style, the author involves the reader within a personal experience of venues from
the Legacy of Rome to theatres of the Renaissance and Eighteenth Century Baroque and
the Gustavian Theatres of Stockholm. His performance experiences include Wagner in
Beyreuth, the Pleasures of Tivoli and Wayang in Singapore. This is a 'must have' title for
those who are as "incurably stagestruck" as the author.

Through the Viewfinder *Jeremy Hoare* **£21.95** ISBN: 9781904031574
Do you want to be a top television cameraman? Well this is going to help!
Through the Viewfinder is aimed at media students wanting to be top professional television
cameramen – but it will also be of interest to anyone who wants to know what goes on
behind the cameras that bring so much into our homes.
The author takes his own opinionated look at how to operate a television camera based on
23 years' experience looking through many viewfinders for a major ITV network company.
Based on interviews with people he has worked with, all leaders in the profession, the book

is based on their views and opinions and is a highly revealing portrait of what happens behind the scenes in television production from a cameraman's point of view.

Walt Disney Concert Hall – The Backstage Story *Patricia MacKay & Richard Pilbrow* **£28.95** ISBN 1904031234
Spanning the 16-year history of the design and construction of the Walt Disney Concert Hall, this book provides a fresh and detailed behind the scenes story of the design and technology from a variety of viewpoints. This is the first book to reveal the "process" of the design of a concert hall.

Yesterday's Lights – A Revolution Reported *Francis Reid* **£26.95** ISBN 1904031323
Set to help new generations to be aware of where the art and science of theatre lighting is coming from – and stimulate a nostalgia trip for those who lived through the period, Francis Reid's latest book has over 350 pages dedicated to the task, covering the 'revolution' from the fifties through to the present day. Although this is a highly personal account of the development of lighting design and technology and he admits that there are 'gaps', you'd be hard put to find anything of significance missing.

Go to www.etbooks.co.uk for full details of above titles and secure online ordering facilities.